PASSION PLAY

◆

PASSION PLAY

◆

SARAH RUHL

THEATRE COMMUNICATIONS GROUP
NEW YORK
2010

Passion Play is published by Theatre Communications Group, Inc., 520 Eighth Avenue, 24th Floor, New York, NY 10018-4156

This publication is made possible in part with public funds from the New York State Council on the Arts, a State Agency.

TCG books are exclusively distributed to the book trade by Consortium Book Sales and Distribution.

LIBRARY OF CONGRESS CATALOGING-IN-PUBLICATION DATA
Ruhl, Sarah.
Passion play / Sarah Ruhl.—1st ed.
p. cm.
ISBN 978-1-55936-348-8
1. Passion-plays. I. Title.
PS3618.U48P37 2010
812'.6—dc22   2010002157

Book design and composition by Lisa Govan
Cover design by Mark Melnick
Cover painting: *The Fall of the Rebel Angels*, Pieter Brueghel the Elder, copyright © The Gallery Collection / Corbis
First Edition, August 2010
Second Printing, January 2018

This play is for Paula Vogel

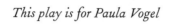

Contents

PLAYWRIGHT'S NOTE

I STARTED WRITING THIS PLAY fourteen years ago after rereading a childhood book which includes an account of Oberammergau in the early 1900s. In this old-fashioned narrative, the man who played Christ was actually so holy as to have become a living embodiment. The woman who played Mary was, in real life, just as pure as the Virgin. I started thinking, how would it shape or misshape a life to play a biblical role year after year? How are we scripted? Where is the line between authentic identity and performance? And is there, in fact, such a line?

The first act is set in 1575 in England, when Queen Elizabeth was about to shut down the Passion Plays in order to control religious representation. Not many towns still performed the Passion in 1575; the village of Act One is, then, itself something of an anachronism, oddly suspended between the Middle Ages and the Renaissance. In 1575, Queen Elizabeth banned religious plays altogether; up until then, more than one hundred towns in the British Isles performed the Passion. Meanwhile, Elizabeth who was excommunicated by the Pope in 1571, increased measures in the 1570s to cleanse England of papal trappings, including Jesuits. Ordinary Catholics often housed priests in what they called "priest holes" in order to maintain Catholic rites.

The second act moves to Oberammergau, Germany—a town where the Passion Play, begun in the Middle Ages, even now continues to be played every ten years. Many narratives describe Oberammergau as a living picture of the New Testament, ignoring the fact that, in 1934, the director of the Passion was already a member of the Nazi party. The actor who played Christ and the actress who played the Virgin Mary were also early party members. By 1947, every actor in the play had at one time been a Nazi, with the exception of the men who played, ironically, Judas and Pontius Pilate. (My play takes liberties with these historical facts.) As late as 1946, the village of Oberammergau denied knowing anything about concentration camps, although Dachau (where Oberammergau's one Jew was sent during the war) was only seventy-five miles away.

The Passion Play, which often incited pogroms during Easter when performed in medieval Germany, became a historical perversion during the war. In 1934, Hitler saw the Passion and was greeted with open arms. He came a second time on August 13, 1934—six weeks after "Night of the Long Knives," when Hitler purged his leadership of homosexuals, Communists and Jews. Act Two of *Passion Play* quotes the nineteenth-century Oberammergau script (famous for its anti-Semitism), as well as quoting a speech Hitler made at a dinner, expressing his admiration for the Oberammergau Passion in 1942. Everything else in the play is an invention. I am indebted to Saul Friedman and James Shapiro for their careful research.

It should be said that, since the war, Oberammergau has made attempts to reform its Passion Play; has invited Jewish scholars and has revised the text in order to reflect a more ecumenical view. Many Passion Plays have enlisted the Anti-Defamation League to get it right, or at least, *more* right. And yet, even today, we are plunged into the same kind of moral/aesthetic debates, as when Mel Gibson took up the mantle of the Passion with his *Passion of the Christ*, which had one of the biggest viewerships, ironically, in the Arab world. But more people talked about "Passion dollars"—the surprise commercial success of the movie—than they did about the dangers of focusing the Gospel story on violent scapegoating.

Years after beginning Parts One and Two of *Passion Play* (which I began with the encouragement of Paula Vogel), I returned to the cycle. I discovered that there was a Passion Play in Spearfish, South Dakota, started by an actor from Germany in the 1940s. I felt that I had to continue the story. Serendipitously, Arena Stage in Washington, D.C., asked me to write a play about America, and I figured that there's nothing more American than the nexus of religion, politics and the theater. Especially when it seemed as if we were in the midst of an unacknowledged holy war, conducted by a man who felt himself to be appointed by God (he must have been appointed by someone, he wasn't appointed by the popular vote in 2000). Never had the medieval world and the digital age seemed so oddly conjoined. I found myself fascinated by how leaders use, misuse and legislate religion for their own political aims, and how leaders turn themselves into theatrical icons. Queen Elizabeth, wearing layers and layers of makeup, "married" herself to England; Hitler took photographs of himself gesticulating until he got it right; Ronald Reagan had miraculous and natural powers as an actor. But what is the difference between acting as performance and acting as moral action? It is no accident that we refer to *theaters of war*.

More and more, it seems to me that the separation between church and state is coming into question in our country. We are a divided nation. And the more divided we are, the less we talk about what divides us. The left is perceived of as antireligious, ideological secularists; the right as religious zealots. But whatever happened to the founding fathers' rationale for separating church and state? More devotion was possible, and more kinds of devotion would be possible, the less the state controlled religious rhetoric. More devotion, and more *conversation* about devotion, would be possible with that freedom. I miss that conversation, and I think theater is a good place for it. To my mind, devotion is like a quality of light—how is it possible to legislate the quality of light? It would be like legislating the invisible moments that happen in a theater. And, ultimately, this play is about those moments—about how actors wring moments out of their private lives in order to bear witness in the community.

Ideally, *Passion Play* (Parts One, Two and Three) would be performed all together in one evening (it should run about three hours plus intermissions) or else in rotating repertory. Together, the three parts form a cycle play—alone, they do something different, but they can technically stand alone. If done in repertory, I suggest doing Parts One and Two on one night, and Part Three on the next. If the resources of one theater are too limited to produce the entire cycle, I can imagine two theaters in one city collaborating to put up the cycle together. In the original guild productions of the Passion, the carpenters in the village would handle the Crucifixion scene and the bakers would handle the Last Supper. Perhaps our theatrical communities could borrow from the primitive guild model.

I wrote the first draft of *Passion Play*, Part Three before the 2004 election, with a great sense of urgency. It's easy to feel powerless as the great political wheels turn, financed by enormous wealth. But then I thought about what starts every grass-roots movement—people organizing in one room. Luckily that very special right is protected by our Constitution. And as ill-suited as some theater artists are to some meanings of the word "organization," there is one thing we tend to do well, and that is to organize people to come to one room. It is not that the play you are about to read is a political treatise—not at all—but it does provide us with another occasion to be in one room together as we continue to meditate on the relationship of community to political icons. And to meditate on what we can do to effect change in very solemn times indeed.

PASSION PLAY

◆

PRODUCTION HISTORY

An early version of *Passion Play* was produced in workshop at the Tristan Bates Theatre in London in July 2002. It was directed by Mark Wing-Davey; the design was by Madeline Herbert and the lighting design was by Emma Chapman. The cast was as follows:

PONTIUS	Colin Tierney / Tim Welton
JOHN	Oliver Chris / Oliver Dimsdale / Paul Ready
MARY I	Kate Maravan
MARY 2	Annabel Capper
VISITING FRIAR, ENGLISHMAN	Alan Cox
VILLAGE IDIOT	Liz White / Nathalie Armin / Hayley Carmichael
CARPENTER I	Peter Warnock / Michael Gilroy
CARPENTER 2	Patrick Brennan / Morgan James
DIRECTOR	David Stevens
MACHINIST, GERMAN OFFICER	Tim Welton / James Albrecht
QUEEN ELIZABETH, HITLER, REAGAN	Scott Handy / Catherine Tate
SHEPHERD	Danny Sapani / James Albrecht
SHEPHERDESS, BIRD	Louise Bolton
OLD LADY	Rita Davies

Passion Play received its world premiere at Arena Stage (Molly Smith, Artistic Director; Edgar Dobie, Managing Director) in Washington, D.C., on September 2, 2005. It was directed by Molly Smith; the set design was by Scott Bradley, the costume design was by Linda Cho, the lighting design was by Joel Moritz, the sound design and original music were by André Pluess; the dramaturg was Mark Bly and the stage manager was Amber Dickerson. The cast was as follows:

PONTIUS, FOOT SOLDIER, P, ENSEMBLE	Felix Solis
JOHN, ERIC, J, ENSEMBLE	Howard W. Overshown
MARY 1, ENSEMBLE	Kelly Brady
MARY 2, ENSEMBLE	Carla Harting
VISITING FRIAR, VISITING ENGLISHMAN, VA 1, ENSEMBLE	Edward James Hyland
VILLAGE IDIOT, VIOLET, ENSEMBLE	Polly Noonan
CARPENTER 1, VA 2, ENSEMBLE	J. Fred Shiffman
CARPENTER 2, ENSEMBLE	Lawrence Redmond
DIRECTOR, ENSEMBLE	Leo Erickson
MACHINIST, GERMAN OFFICER, YOUNG DIRECTOR, ENSEMBLE	Karl Miller
QUEEN ELIZABETH, HITLER, REAGAN, NIXON, ENSEMBLE	Robert Dorfman
ENSEMBLE	Parker Dixon

Passion Play was produced at the Goodman Theatre (Robert Falls, Artistic Director; Roche Schulfer, Executive Director) in Chicago on September 15, 2007. It was directed by Mark Wing-Davey; the set design was by Allen Moyer, the costume design was by Gabriel Berry, the lighting design was by James F. Ingalls, the sound design was by Cecil Averett, the projection design was by Ruppert Bohle; the dramaturg was Tanya Palmer, the production stage manager was Joseph Drummond and the stage manager was T. Paul Lynch. The cast was as follows:

PONTIUS THE FISH GUTTER, FOOT SOLDIER, P	Brian Sgambati
JOHN THE FISHERMAN, ERIC, J	Joaquín Torres
MARY 1	Kristen Bush

MARY 2	Nicole Wiesner
VISITING FRIAR, VISITING ENGLISHMAN,	
YOUNG DIRECTOR	Alan Cox
VILLAGE IDIOT, VIOLET	Polly Noonan
CARPENTER 1, TOWNSMAN	Brendan Averett
CARPENTER 2, TOWNSMAN	Keith Kupferer
DIRECTOR	Craig Spidle
MACHINIST, GERMAN OFFICER, VA	John Hoogenakker
QUEEN ELIZABETH, HITLER,	
REAGAN	T. Ryder Smith
ENSEMBLE	Tiffany Bedwell, Jeremy Clark, Kyle Lemieux, Ron Rains, Jayce Ryan

Passion Play was produced at Yale Repertory Theatre (James Bundy, Artistic Director; Victoria Nolan, Managing Director) in New Haven, CT, on September 19, 2008. It was directed by Mark Wing-Davey; the set design was by Allen Moyer, the costume design was by Ilona Somogyi, the lighting design was by Stephen Strawbridge, the sound design was by Charles Coes; the production dramaturg was Colin Mannex and the stage manager was James Mountcastle. The cast was as follows:

PONTIUS THE FISH GUTTER	Felix Solis
JOHN THE FISHERMAN	Joaquín Torres
MARY 1	Susan Pourfar
MARY 2	Nicole Wiesner
VISITING FRIAR, VISITING ENGLISHMAN, VA	Thomas Jay Ryan
VILLAGE IDIOT, VIOLET	Polly Noonan
CARPENTER 1	Brendan Averett
CARPENTER 2	Austin Durant
DIRECTOR	Keith Reddin
MACHINIST, GERMAN OFFICER,	
YOUNG DIRECTOR	Dieterich Gray
QUEEN ELIZABETH, HITLER, REAGAN	Kathleen Chalfant
ENSEMBLE	Laura Esposito, Brian Hastert, Slate Holmgren, Barret O'Brien, Luke Robertson

Passion Play was produced by Epic Theatre Ensemble (Zak Berkman, Melissa Friedman, Ron Russell; Executive Directors) at The Irondale Center in Brooklyn, NY, on May 12, 2010. It was directed by Mark Wing-Davey; the set design was by Warren Karp and Allen Moyer, the costume design was by Gabriel Berry and Antonia Ford-Roberts, the lighting design was by David Weiner, additional music was composed by David Van Tieghem; the associate director was Scott Illingworth, the movement director was James Calder; the fight director was David Anzuelo, the dialect coach was Deborah Hecht and the stage manager was Iris O'Brien. The cast was as follows:

PONTIUS THE FISH GUTTER	Dominic Fumusa
JOHN THE FISHERMAN	Hale Appleman
MARY 1	Kate Turnbull
MARY 2	Nicole Wiesner
VISITING FRIAR, VISITING ENGLISHMAN	Daniel Pearce
VILLAGE IDIOT, VIOLET	Polly Noonan
CARPENTER 1	Brendan Averett
CARPENTER 2	Godfrey L. Simmons, Jr.
DIRECTOR	Keith Reddin
MACHINIST, GERMAN OFFICER, YOUNG DIRECTOR	Alex Podulke
QUEEN ELIZABETH, HITLER, REAGAN	T. Ryder Smith

Character Breakdown for the Entire Cycle

The full play requires eleven actors. Each actor retains a semblance of his or her role when the play jumps in time and space. For example, Pontius the Fish Gutter becomes a Foot Soldier in Part Two and a Vietnam vet named "P" in Part Three. There is some flexibility in how the Carpenters and Machinist are reincarnated in Part Three. The play is an ensemble piece, and all the players help to create the world of the play within the play.

Part One *England, 1575*	*Part Two* *Germany, 1934*	*Part Three* *South Dakota, 1969–the present*
PONTIUS THE FISH GUTTER (plays Pontius Pilate and Satan)	FOOT SOLDIER (plays Pontius Pilate)	P (plays Pontius Pilate and Satan)
JOHN THE FISHERMAN (plays Jesus and Adam)	ERIC (plays Jesus)	J (plays Jesus)
MARY 1 (plays the Virgin Mary and Eve)	ELSA (plays the Virgin Mary)	MARY 1 (plays the Virgin Mary)
MARY 2 (plays Mary Magdalen)	MARY 2 (plays Mary Magdalen)	MARY 2 (plays Mary Magdalen)
VISITING FRIAR	VISITING ENGLISHMAN, SIMON LILY	VA PSYCHIATRIST
VILLIAGE IDIOT	VIOLET	VIOLET

Part One *England, 1575*	Part Two *Germany, 1934*	Part Three *South Dakota,* *1969–the present*
CARPENTER 1, SAM (plays the angel Gabriel)	CARPENTER 1, JOHANN	CARPENTER 1/ ENSEMBLE
CARPENTER 2, SIMON (plays Joseph)	CARPENTER 2, LUDWIG	CARPENTER 2/ ENSEMBLE
DIRECTOR	DIRECTOR, ROCHUS SCHALLHAMMER	DIRECTOR
MACHINIST (plays an emperor)	GERMAN OFFICER	YOUNG DIRECTOR
QUEEN ELIZABETH	HITLER	PRESIDENT REAGAN, QUEEN ELIZABETH, HITLER

PASSION PLAY

A Village in Northern England, Spring, 1575

◆

Characters

PONTIUS THE FISH GUTTER	plays Pontius Pilate and Satan
JOHN THE FISHERMAN	plays Jesus and Adam
MARY 1	plays the Virgin Mary and Eve
MARY 2	plays Mary Magdalen
VISITING FRIAR	
VILLAGE IDIOT	
CARPENTER 1 OR SAM	plays the angel Gabriel
CARPENTER 2 OR SIMON	plays Joseph
DIRECTOR	
MACHINIST	plays an emperor
QUEEN ELIZABETH	preferably a man in drag

Set

The suggestion of the sea.
A playing space.

PROLOGUE

CHORUS

We make our play in England
in the north
by the sea
in the open air of England.
The Virgin Queen is on her throne
the Catholics are mostly done.
Take pity on our simple play—
we've no fancy lights
only the bare light of day.
The good Lord tells us,
to be most simple is to be most good
so here is honest rough-hewn wood.
We ask you, dear audience, to use your eyes, ears,
your most inward sight
for here is day *(a painted sun)*
and here is night *(a painted moon)*.
And now, the play.

SCENE 1: BUILDING THE ROOD

A man on a cross. The sound of sawing.
At first we are not sure whether or not this is a real crucifixion.
Carpenter 1, Sam, measures John the Fisherman from head to toe.

CARPENTER I

You have g—grown.

JOHN

I'm afraid so. I wish my bones would not make such work for you year after year.

CARPENTER I

You cannot stop your bones from gr-gr—growing.

JOHN

My cousin's bones stopped growing three years ago, and his bones have troubled no seamstress with new stitches since. Perhaps he should play my part.

CARPENTER 2

Oh, but he's a limp wee little thing. Gutted his own hand when he meant to gut a flounder. And now his back's as crooked as the road to hell!

JOHN

Now you mustn't make fun of poor Pontius.

CARPENTER 1

What mmmm mighty arms you have! You could swing many a fi-fi-fine lady on those br-brawny arms.

JOHN

You could knock me down easily, Sam!

CARPENTER 1

Nnno. I would never hhhurt my John boy.

CARPENTER 2

Now me and him may be twins, but we're as different as two peas in different pods. He likes his ale light, I like it dark. He likes Sundays, I detest 'em. I like blonds, and he likes his brunettes, don't you there, Sam?

The Sky Turns Red.

JOHN

Why there's that red light again!

CARPENTER 2

So it is! What the devil . . .

CARPENTER 1

It's been a creeping and a cr-cr-crawling into the cracks in the windows! It makes me afffraid.

They stand, transfixed. The light disperses and becomes natural.

CARPENTER 2

Oh well, I suppose the sun must be angry about something. Only one more little nail.

He pounds in a nail.

There. Your measurements, my good man, have been taken.

He helps John off the cross.
Exit Carpenter 1 and John.
Carpenter 2 stays behind to tell the audience:

I have blisters and splinters and all for the glory of God. My father's father was a carpenter. My father's father's father was a carpenter. We all have blisters and splinters in our fingers and all for the glory of God.

Scene 2: Pontius and a Traveling Friar

Pontius, to the audience:

PONTIUS
All my life I've wanted to play Christ . . . if only, I thought, they put me on a cross, I would feel holy, I would walk upright. And every year my cousin plays the Savior.

I want to kill my cousin. No—I want—when he is on the cross—and if I left him on just the slightest bit too long—and if the pretend nails were real . . . then they would nail me to the cross, and I would follow him to glory.

My cousin is a good man—ah, the tingling in my head again—something pulling—like a string at the top—a puppet—up down up down, string.

Today the sky turned red, the sky turned red, and we should kneel down and take notice but everyone's too busy eating their bloody porridge!

16

On the other side of the stage, a Visiting Friar appears.
He is in disguise.

VISITING FRIAR

(Addressing the audience) Today I walked far and far until I noticed that the shrubbery had changed and I was out of my province. And then—the sky turned red! At two in the afternoon! If shivers didn't crawl up and down my spine like worms . . .

PONTIUS

(To the audience) My cousin is nothing but a bastard!

VISITING FRIAR

(To the audience) I will conceal myself behind a tree and observe this young man.

PONTIUS

(To the audience) He is a thorn in my side that must be plucked out. If I were a woman I could bake this malice into my bread, but as it is, I am a man and I must make this malice a knife. I will store my acorns of malice, I will guard them and I will harvest them in the spring.

(Pontius notices the Visiting Friar and changes his face) Hello, traveler! What brings you to our little town? New faces are seldom seen here.

VISITING FRIAR

I come from a neighboring village but am tired and require water. Are you not the famed village that plays the Passion, scattering tales of its holiness across the land?

PONTIUS

We are that very village, sir.

VISITING FRIAR

Not many towns dare in these dark days to play the Passion in England.

PONTIUS

Aye. This town is slow to change.

VISITING FRIAR

Are you then the same town famed for a most beautiful and graceful young man who plays the part of Christ?

PONTIUS

He is, in point of fact—my cousin.

VISITING FRIAR

Your family must be proud of such a relation.

PONTIUS

My family is very proud of my cousin, I'm sure.

A grimace to the audience. A smile to the Visiting Friar.

VISITING FRIAR

And you? What do you play?

PONTIUS

Pontius Pilate—and Satan.

VISITING FRIAR

Ah! To be sure!

Pontius grimaces to the audience. A smile to the Friar.

PONTIUS

Would you like to take a drink of water at my home?

VISITING FRIAR

I would be most grateful. Perhaps I can meet the famed cousin of yours.

PONTIUS

By all means!
(To the audience) Between gritted teeth, between bloody gritted teeth!

SCENE 3: JOHN THE FISHERMAN'S KITCHEN, DAY

VISITING FRIAR
You're just as comely and upright as they say.

JOHN
Thank you.

VISITING FRIAR
With the same dimple in the chin.

JOHN
You must be hungry. Can I make you some eggs, sir?

VISITING FRIAR
I would be honored to eat an egg made by your holy hands.
(Checking the door, in low tones) Young man, can I trust you're a
Catholic?

JOHN
We are all Catholic in our private hearts though we have no public
house of worship left. The stage is our house of worship.

19

The Visiting Friar takes off his disguise, revealing a priest's cowl.
John kneels down and kisses the hand of the Friar.

God save you! Is it not dangerous for you to stay here? Are they not catching priests and putting them into prison?

VISITING FRIAR

Aye. We're hidden in closets and priest holes all over England.

JOHN

And are you now in need of a hiding place?

VISITING FRIAR

Aye. But I would not dream of putting you in danger.

JOHN

Stay with us.

VISITING FRIAR

I know now why they tell tales of your Christ. You have His spirit.

JOHN

You really mustn't believe such things, good Friar. Perhaps you'd like to come to our rehearsal today. You could see the scaffolds that lift men up, the machinery that brings men down. You'll see that I'm no better than the tattered costume that I wear.

VISITING FRIAR

I would be honored to see the famed village rehearse.

SCENE 4: THE VILLAGE IDIOT

Day. The heavenly choir rehearses.
The Director conducts, and arranges their halos.
The Visiting Friar watches.
The Village Idiot sits cross-legged in the town square,
playing with a jack-in-the-box.
The sound of a musical jack-in-the-box crank.

VILLAGE IDIOT

In a time, in a time, in a time without . . . words—oh—pop—pop
goes the weasel! *(Laughs)* You have a strange ugly face, surprising
to pop out at me! Why do you pop out at me? Do you like me, scary
big nose? *(Laughs again)*

DIRECTOR

Shut your mouth, village idiot!

VILLAGE IDIOT

(To the jack-in-the-box) Well, Jack, Big Director Man told us to shut
our mouths—I shut your mouth. *(Stuffs him back in box)* Now
I want you out again to play with. *(Winding)* Bird of a heart, heart

21

of a giant, big beast in the mouth of hell! Pop! Jack! You again—darling Jack, I thought I'd never see you again, shut down in that dark, dark box, your body all bent and twisted. *(Kisses him)* I'm sorry I put you in your box, dear Jack . . .

DIRECTOR

(Overlapping slightly) I said, shut your mouth, village idiot! The heavenly choir rehearses!

VILLAGE IDIOT

The heavenly choir rehearses, oh, oh, the heavenly choir rehearses . . . no part for Jack or me, oh no. You just pop out of a box, don't you, Jack? And I just wind you because things need to be wound—clocks—tick tick—hearts—tick tick—oh! Beautiful, beautiful Jack with your heart in a box.

The Director marches over and ties the Village Idiot to a stump, putting the jack-in-the-box a distance away.

Ahhhh! JACK! SAVE ME! It is dark and I am in the box . . . I'll close my eyes and make the sky turn red . . . now . . . now . . .

The Sky Turns Red.
The heavenly choir stops singing.
The heavenly choir looks up.

See that, Jack! Did you see?

Scene 5: Mary and Mary

The Director and the half naked figure of John the Fisherman
practice the Crucifixion scene.
The Visiting Friar looks on in disguise.
Mary 1 and Mary 2 sit on the other side of the stage under a tree.
Mary 1 wears a halo.

MARY 2
Mary Magdalen was a whore because she pretended and that's like
me—I'm a whore because I pretend things.

MARY 1
How do you know Mary Magdalen pretended things?

MARY 2
I don't know. I just know.

MARY 1
Oh, his acting is divine! Oh! Oh! His loincloth is slipping!

MARY 2

It is easy and fun to seduce men—you can pretend things, and it's
fun to pretend—but then you have to bed them, and that is the boring part—you can hardly pretend anything interesting with your
legs apart.

MARY 1

Boring! Why, Mary, your brain is addled. Milking cows is boring.
Needlework is boring.

MARY 2

It's all one! At least with needlework, *I* work the needle and stitch
where I please instead of lying like a tapestry only to be pricked. At
least with cow-milking *I* squeeze the teet instead of standing
swollen and mooing.

MARY 1

No, no, Mary. You can't possibly think milking cows and needlework and men-bedding are all one. Perhaps you've not found the
right man.

MARY 2

Perhaps.

MARY 1

John the Fisherman, for instance, he's handsome and true. And seeing him so oft in his rehearsal loincloth—it makes me pound and
pound.

MARY 2

I've known John the Fisherman too long to fancy him in a loincloth.
I like to stick to my books. There's a heap more amusement in one
book than in a score of beddings all alike.

MARY 1

And his muscles like a lion's, and golden too!

MARY 2

Hmmph.

Mary 1 freezes, ogling John the Fisherman. Mary 2 turns to the audience:

When I was a child I noticed one day that all the girls turned into strange flapping birds when the boys walked by. Their eyes got huge and acquired wings, as though cursed, wings for eyelashes to flutter and flap. I thought the wings on their eyes might fly them to a different land altogether. I didn't turn into a bird around anyone—I stayed quiet and very still.

MARY 1

Oh! Oh! His loincloth is slipping!

MARY 2

It's sinful to covet your own son, Mary. It's a sin, a sin against God.

MARY 1

I didn't ask to play his mother.

MARY 2

I'm sure it's not right, Mary.
Perhaps we should switch roles.
I think my part has more scenes with John the Fisherman.

MARY 1

Oh!

MARY 2

Run find the director and ask! Go on!

Mary 1 runs off.

(Looking after Mary 1) Yes, much better to play the Virgin Mary— to have a baby—yes—I do like babies—and a husband—yes, I do like men—I do—but not to bed the one to get the other! No won-

der she smiled so tenderly in all the paintings. The happiest and best of women.

Enter the Director and Mary 1.

DIRECTOR

I'm sorry, ladies, but you've signed your contracts. And besides, *you* look like a saint *(To Mary 1)* and *you (Points to Mary 2)* look like a whore. There's no getting around it. *(To Mary 2)* Look at that beauty mark and that gap between the teeth. And you've got a bit of a deformity in the chin—it just wouldn't do for the Virgin Mary to have a bit of deformity in the chin. *(To Mary 1)* And her smile. A smile like that would melt the devil's heart. But not mine. Now finish memorizing your parts, ladies. There's no time for all of this driveling anarchy.

Enter the Visiting Friar, in disguise.

VISITING FRIAR

Would anyone here like to confess their sins?

MARY 2

I would.

VISITING FRIAR

Meet me around the corner after dark.

Scene 6: At the Confessional

MARY 2

Forgive me Father, for I have sinned. I have dreams of women embracing me and kissing me full on the lips.

VISITING FRIAR

That is indeed a sin. I want you to say twenty Hail Marys, thirty-two Our Fathers, and hang a crucifix above your bed.

MARY 2

But there is a crucifix above my bed, Father. And I find that I rather enjoy the dreams, though I try not to have them.

VISITING FRIAR

Now you mustn't enjoy such dreams, Mary. It addles a young girl's brain to play the role of a whore from a young age. I want you to say your penances, chew on a gingerroot, and change parts with the shepherdess.

MARY 2

Oh, but she's not half so good as me, Father. I'll be good, so good!
I'm good at pretending!

VISITING FRIAR

Now, Mary, I am looking after the salvation of your soul.

MARY 2

Yes, Father. *(Pause)* Father, why is it wrong to dream of women
kissing you full on the lips?

VISITING FRIAR

Ask God, Mary. Only God can explain, only God—the Father.

The Sky Turns Red.

MARY 2

Oh the sky, the sky, again the sky!

Scene 7

Pontius sits on a stoop, cleaning his shoes with a knife.

PONTIUS

Last night the moon threw its head back, laughing at me—a white wedge—a laughing pitchfork—and tonight the moon sank down on his haunches—his face turned full at me—he looked bewildered and afraid. Had the fat white face of a dunce. You think I'm a bloody fool to speak of the moon, but who else will be a witness to my grief?

The doctor who birthed me, see, he didn't sew up my belly properly. Most people have got some skin between their guts and the air of the world, not me, not me. You can stick your finger way into my belly button, and when you pull it out it smells like gangrene, like fish.

I gut the fish. My cousin—he catches 'em. He don't have to see their innards. He don't have to talk to dead fish all day. He can talk to the sea. Me—I close my nose and I smell the stench of dead fish. I close my eyes and see dead fish coming at me in a parade.

He closes his eyes and huge beautiful fish puppets walk toward him as if in a parade. They surround him and undress him until he wears only a loincloth. They leave to the beating of drums. He turns to the audience. He blinks. The sound of the sea gurgles.

SCENE 8: NIGHT

Mary 1 kneels by her bed.

Hail Mary, full of grace . . .

(To the audience) I hate to sleep alone. My feet get cold. I put socks on and then my feet get hot so I take them off under the blankets but then my feet get cold again in the night.

(Putting her socks on) It's unnatural, cold and unnatural, this solitary sleeping. The sheep sleep together, all woolly and warm. I get too lonesome to sleep alone. I slept with my parents till I got too old. One time they locked me out—I could hear why—strange sounds coming from the bed. When I got old enough I found men to sleep with—men with hair on their legs and bellies to keep me warm at night. I go out walking sometimes to find them.

She climbs down a rope and out of her window.

I've never been with child. Don't know why. Better not to ask God.

John the Fisherman out walking in a shaft of light.

JOHN

Sometimes—tonight—a feeling of grace comes and I feel peaceful and easy and ready to die but still aware of the moon's beauty, like silver fish scales shedding. Skin covers the world—luminous moon-skin—and I must step softly and slowly on it—the cobbled streets have fish skin, the trees have human skin—and it is not fearsome, only slow and lovely and soft, but I must be careful not to prick you and make you bleed.

Mary 1 walks toward him, carrying a jar.

MARY I

Good evening.

JOHN

Good evening, Mary. What brings you into the night air by yourself?

MARY I

Uuum . . . My mother—she's sick—doctor told me to trap the night air in a jar and bring it back to her.

JOHN

May I help?

Mary looks down, embarrassed.

MARY I

Umm—

JOHN

I'd do anything to help you and your good mother, Mary.

MARY I

Could you climb up that wagon, John, and trap that particular spot of air?

She hands him a jar and he climbs an abstracted wagon.

JOHN

This spot?

She scrutinizes him from behind.

MARY 1

Perhaps a little to the left.
And to the right. And up. Yes, that bit there.

JOHN
(Handing her the jar) I hope this will do, Mary.

She smiles at him.

Your mother . . . is she very sick?

MARY 1

My mother? . . . oh yes . . . her belly . . . she swallowed something . . .

JOHN
I'm sorry, Mary. You know I would drink your sorrow if I could.

John escorts Mary 1 offstage.
Pontius appears from behind a bush.

PONTIUS

Always, always, always him!

I can cry
only out of one eye.
Only the left
and the right stays dry.
Dry as a bone
dry as a cunt
who's left alone.
Oh, God let me cry!

Out of both eyes, please God,
please God let me cry!

Same scene. Night.

Mary 1 climbs back into her bedroom window.

MARY I
It will be a cold bed for me again tonight. He's chaste as a clam.

Scene 9: The Fall of Man — A Rehearsal

Mary 1, the Director, Pontius and an apple.

DIRECTOR
In this scene, Mary, you are tempted by a delicious, ripe fruit. Your mouth should water. Now. Go.

PONTIUS
(As Satan) Eve! Eve!

MARY I
(As Eve) Who is there?

PONTIUS
I, a friend.
And for thy good is the coming.
Bite on boldly, be not abashed.

DIRECTOR
Don't be afraid, Pontius. Slink your skinny arm around her waist. There, there. Dangle the apple in front of her lips.

> MARY I

Then will I to thy teaching trust,
And fang this fruit unto our food.

She bites timidly into the apple.

> DIRECTOR

Bite harder! The juice must dribble down your chin! Again!

> MARY I

Then will I to thy teaching trust,
And fang this fruit unto our food.

She bites the apple, hard, a large section of apple in her mouth.

> PONTIUS

Oh!

> DIRECTOR

Good.

Scene 10: Night

Pontius sits on a wagon, looking at stars.

PONTIUS
(To the audience) I gutted a fish today—I thought it was dead—I slit open its belly—and five live fishes squirmed out. They stunk of death. They wriggled and wraggled in the guts of their mother and they died one by one. The last one to go was a real wriggler. He watched everyone go before him—he swam around in their fishy guts—and then I slammed the knife down on his back. I couldn't stand to see one so alone and so alive, so I killed the poor devil to put it out of its misery.

He sees Mary 1 offstage.

Hush—Mary walks. The smell of the moon follows her. And her eyes follow my cousin. Would she kiss a poor fishmonger? Would she wrap her arms around the stench?

Mary 1 appears, holding a jar.

Miss Mary, why are you out walking at this time of night?

MARY I

You startled me.

PONTIUS

I didn't mean to frighten you, Mary.

MARY I

There is little light from the moon tonight. The trees cast their shadows on your face.

PONTIUS

I can see you. I can see you because I have studied your face in the dark of my bed before sleeping.

MARY I

I am a Christian woman.

PONTIUS

Why are you out walking tonight?

He comes closer to her.

MARY I

You smell of fish.

PONTIUS

I slit open their bellies all day. Why are you out walking tonight?

MARY I

I could sell you some rose water. You could sprinkle it over your hands.

PONTIUS

Oh, would you Miss Mary?

MARY I

Well . . . yes. Good night.

She turns to go.

PONTIUS

Don't go.

(To the audience) She is a deer wrapped in brown velvet. She is the air breathing inside the body of a violin.

(To her) Don't go.

MARY I

It's late.

PONTIUS

According to who? The sun? The moon? It's early for the sun—he hasn't even woken from his nap. And it's only mid-afternoon for the moon, she's just barely risen. And you out walking . . . Owls don't fly out of their dens for no reason.

MARY I

You play tricks with words.

PONTIUS

Do you play tricks, Mary?

MARY I

Certainly not.

They look at each other. He seizes her. They kiss. She drops the jar.

The night air. You've spilled it.

Pontius gets on the wagon
and traps the same bit of air that John has trapped.
He gives it to her.
She pities him. Kisses him.

You don't taste like other men.

PONTIUS

I know.

She kisses him again.

MARY 1

They would take away my part or worse if they knew.

PONTIUS

I will be silent as a dead fish, silent as a closed box under water.

They kiss.
Strange watery noises.

SCENE 11

The Village Idiot wakes up from a dream, frightened.

VILLAGE IDIOT

Jack! I thought I had me a dream of the Queen. Why, she was standing up in heaven, and she was naked and pregnant—full pregnant, swollen like a melon. Her belly was dangling over her private parts, which were flaming red. They say the privates are the same color as the eyebrows but you never can say with certainty until you've given 'em a thorough look. But I blushed, I did, to see the Queen's privates—they're always covered up with drapes and curtains like a stage. So the Queen, she looks at me, with a real cold glimmer in her eyes like jewels, and she says, "I have come to stop the Passion." And she points her bony little finger at me, and I wake up, breathing heavy and scared-like.

Scene 12: In the Forest

Mary 1 and Mary 2. The shadows of trees on their faces.

MARY 2

How long?

MARY 1

Too long.

MARY 2

Big?

MARY 1

A little.

MARY 2

In your costume?

MARY 1

Not yet.

MARY 2

Christ.

MARY 1

Yes.

MARY 2

You could be killed.

MARY 1

Don't.

MARY 2

Vomit?

MARY 1

Yes.

MARY 2

Breasts?

MARY 1

Yes. I think so.

MARY 2

Holy Mother of God.

MARY 1

Please.

MARY 2

You have to leave.

MARY 1

NO!

MARY 2

What, then?

MARY 1

I want my part.

MARY 2

There's a woman in a neighboring village . . .

MARY 1

No!

MARY 2

What then, what?

MARY 1

I don't know.

MARY 2

In one month . . .

MARY 1

I know. But I want my part.

MARY 2

I know you do, Mary.

MARY 1

Please.

Don't tell.

MARY 2

Yes, of course.

MARY 1

The woman in the neighboring village . . . does she?

MARY 2

Yes.

MARY 1

I'll wait. Two weeks.

MARY 2

I'd like to kill him.

MARY 1

I fear, Mary, sometimes I fear . . .

MARY 2

What is it?

MARY 1

I dream, night after night, that I give birth to a fish . . . a huge, ugly, dead fish with a gaping mouth.

SCENE 13: THE FLYING MACHINE

A rehearsal. The Machinist, Director, Mary 1, Mary 2, Carpenter 1 and Carpenter 2. Carpenter 1 plays the angel Gabriel.

MACHINIST

The flying machinist's profession is closer to God than any. What is the one power denied to man by God? God gave us fire, God gave us water. We can talk, walk, swim, screw until we're blue in the face. But who wants to swim in the bloody cold water, shivering and stinking like pond scum when you could fly through the treetops? But who among us can fly? Huh? Tell me!

And who among us doesn't want to fly? Who among you has never dreamed of flying, of skimming the honey stalks with your noses? Of flying like water bugs over ponds and taking in the stench?

But who among us has flown? None! None! And who among us knows how to make a man fly?

Pause.

Me! So shut your bloody traps and listen to me!

I'm going to rig you up by the seat of your pants, and do you know what you're going to do? You are going to fly like a bird like an insect with golden wings like an angel! I've worked with the best of them—I've worked with Simon Daybell, with Martinius Lily, with SEBASTIAN MONK—and none of them—*none*—has ever rigged an angel the way I rig 'em.
Now strap this on.

Carpenter 1 straps on a harness.

VILLAGE IDIOT
(Eyes closed, holding her jack-in-the-box tightly to her chest) And lo, the angel of the Lord came upon them, and the glory of the Lord shone round about them, and they were sore afraid.

Carpenter 1 shouts as he's rigged up the machine.

MACHINIST
Shut your mouth, will you? Do angels scream when they fly? No, by Christ, they like flying! They bloody love it!

Carpenter 1 dangles. Mary 1, meanwhile, looks ill.

DIRECTOR
(To Carpenter 1) There. Now say the bloody line. And you. *(Points to Carpenter 2, who is dressed as Joseph)* Kneel down. Look surprised.

Carpenter 2 looks surprised.

Not surprised like you've wet yourself. Surprised as in amazed. Surprised holy-like. Surprised like your wife's bosom has grown big as two pumpkins, all at once.

Carpenter 2 opens his mouth wide.

There. Continue.

CARPENTER 1 *(As Gabriel)*	VILLAGE IDIOT
Hail, thou that art	Hail, thou that art
highly f-favored,	highly favored,
the Lord is with thee, Mary.	the Lord is with thee, JACK.
Bb-lessed art thou among	Blessed art thou among
women.	women.

DIRECTOR

(To Mary 1) What's wrong with you? Look surprised. Look happy.
Look radiant.

MARY 1

Yes, sir.

DIRECTOR

Joseph—let's have your line.

CARPENTER 2

She is with child, I know not how.
Who could trust any woman now?
Hail, Mary!

MARY 1

By God's will, Joseph, must it be.
For certainly save God and ye
I know no other man
Nor in flesh have been defiled.
God knows all my doing.

CARPENTER 1	VILLAGE IDIOT
Behold, M-Mary, thou shalt	Behold, Jack, thou shalt
b-bring forth a son	bring forth a son
and shalt call his name	and shalt call his name
J-Jesus.	JACK.

The Sky Turns Red.
Everyone looks up.
The Machinist loses hold of the flying machine.

CARPENTER I

Oh, the sky!

Carpenter 1's harness falls and he comes crashing down.
He screams.

Scene 14: Mary Visits Pontius at Work

Pontius stands at a counter and guts fish. Sees Mary. Drops his work.
Washes the fish blood off his hands with water from a bucket.

PONTIUS

You.

MARY 1

I need to speak with you.

PONTIUS

I wrote you letters. I scented them with rose water.

MARY 1

Where there are no ears.

PONTIUS

What of my letters? Did you get them? Your eyes hard like flint,
Mary, you're killing me—

MARY I

I said I need to speak with you.

PONTIUS

Come to tell me I smell of fish? We rolled into the earth, Mary. Come to tell me you forgot?

MARY I

I'm pregnant.

PONTIUS

Oh God.

MARY I

And don't take the Lord's name in vain, neither.

PONTIUS

Run away with me, Mary. We'll be a Trinity. You, me, the baby. You can nail me to a cross, Mary, I'm yours, yours forever. You can scourge me every night and still I'm yours forever.

She doesn't speak.

Can I touch?

She nods. Pontius puts his hand on her belly, reverent.

My life in your belly! Oh, it's ticking, Mary! I can hear it! Marry me. Marry everything—the fish guts, the bile—I'll become clean for you, Mary.

MARY I

No.

He takes his hand off her stomach.

PONTIUS

You love him, don't you? That it?

MARY I

I want to keep my part.

PONTIUS

Curse the part, Mary! Curse the part! It's a tiddling, priddling, little turd of a play. Plays aren't real. Your knee on my chest, Mary, that's real. Marry me!

MARY I

Ever since I was little I've wanted to play the Virgin Mary.

PONTIUS

You can pretend you're the Virgin Mary in my bed! You can scream ten Hail Marys in the ecstasies of love. Do you remember how you shuddered?

MARY I

Christ won't love me.

PONTIUS

Which one, Mary? My cousin or the one from the Good Book?

MARY I

Just Christ, Christ himself . . .

PONTIUS

By Christ himself, then, let's run off together—you can have your baby in a manger, the softest hay, your face—honeyed—eyes milky, I'll comb your hair with straw . . . Kiss me, Mary.

MARY I

No.

PONTIUS

Leave my sight or I swear . . . I won't be accountable.

She turns to leave. Turns back.

MARY 1

My wedding dress would turn red.

PONTIUS

What?

MARY 1

Dresses—they know things—you think they don't—they hang so
quietly, but they know things the way you know things and I know
things and they tell—oh, yes.

She looks at him, turns and leaves.
Pontius slams his knife down into the table.

Scene 15: Mary and Mary

MARY 2

I have an idea.

MARY 1

Tell me.

Mary 2 whispers into Mary 1's ear.

Scene 16: At the Confessional

MARY I

There's been a miracle, Father, I wanted to tell you first. God has impregnated me that I can better play the Virgin Mary.

VISITING FRIAR

Child . . .

MARY I

I had a vision, Father. Angels—beautiful angels—calling me, saying, blessed is the fruit of thy womb.

VISITING FRIAR

Sweet Jesus.

MARY I

I was sleeping, but they called to me from the window . . . There was one angel, dressed all in blue, with stars in her hair . . . I felt my belly, and it's become round like a melon since yesterday . . .

VISITING FRIAR

You're quite sure, Mary?

MARY I

Yes.

VISITING FRIAR

Glory be to God. A miracle.

He crosses himself.

MARY I

I feel very honored, of course.

VISITING FRIAR

Never, Mary, never have you . . .

MARY I

No, Father, of course not.

VISITING FRIAR

Are you sure, Mary? Blessedly sure?

MARY I

Yes.

SCENE 17: THE DEATH OF PONTIUS PILATE—
A REHEARSAL

Pontius, the Director, the Machinist, Mary 2 and Carpenter 2.

MACHINIST

(As the Emperor, LOUD) Out on thee, thou rascally fellow!
Thou hast killed Jesus,
My dear Lord.

DIRECTOR

Remember—you are an emperor. Do you know what that means?
Being the emperor means someone else chews your very food for
you. No need to shout. Peasants bend forward to hear you whisper.
Carry on.

MACHINIST

(Whispering) Put this fellow in a dungeon to rot,
That he may see no light at all;
he is a sorcerer.

DIRECTOR

Let's move on. Go ahead, Pontius. Now—you are very distressed
in this scene.

PONTIUS

I well know I shall die:
Great is my anxiety *(Pronounced to rhyme)*
Distressed am I.

DIRECTOR

Use this knife.

The Director gives Pontius a knife.

PONTIUS

So that no man in the world may
Give me a cruel death;
My own heart
With my knife I will pierce—
Oh! Alas and welaway—

He stabs himself with a stage knife.
He dies a long, painful stage death, groaning.
He punctures his eyes, slits open his belly.

DIRECTOR

Good, Pontius. You're improving nicely.

The Visiting Friar enters.

VISITING FRIAR

There's been a miracle. Mary is with child.

Pontius gives the Visiting Friar a wild look.
A tableau.

Scene 18: Mary Is Visited by Jesus

Mary 1 lies in bed. John the Fisherman enters, kneels at her bedside.

JOHN

Bless you, Mary.

MARY 1

No, John, no.

JOHN

A miracle sleeps in your belly.

MARY 1

If anything were to happen to me, would you raise the child? Be its father?

JOHN

Anything for you and the child, Mary.

MARY 1

You believe me, don't you?

JOHN

I would never doubt your word, Mary, or the word of the Lord. You're beautiful. You're radiant with the sweat of the Lord on your brow.

MARY I

I feel it kicking. God's child.

A pause.

JOHN

Marry me. Be my wife. We'll raise the child together as Mary and Joseph did before us. I'll be a good husband, Mary. I'll never touch you, if that's what you want. I'll fish all day—I'll feed us with fruit from the sea.

MARY I

Oh God, that I could, John.

JOHN

I understand, Mary, if you don't fancy me. I'm not worthy of you . . . you have God in your belly.

MARY I

It's not that . . . It's only that . . . I'm God's bride now.

JOHN

I see . . . It's better that way. It's—a miracle.

SCENE 19: THE SCOURGING — A REHEARSAL

Mary 2, Carpenter 1, Carpenter 2, the Machinist and Pontius.

CARPENTER 2

I see where her eye wanders . . . She's a pretty little thing, too pretty
if you ask me.

CARPENTER 1

St-stop. G-god wouldn't like you to speak that way of Ma-mary.

CARPENTER 2

She's been hankering after John the Fisherman all month and perhaps she's finally gotten what she wanted out of him.

MARY 2

(To Carpenter 2) I've seen your lecherous eyes . . . You wish you could
lay a hand on Mary and now she's God's bride, you're jealous.

CARPENTER 2

True enough, I'd like to take Miss Mary to a field somewhere, but
what does that have to do with the price of eggs and butter? So

would every other young lad in this town, and that's *exactly* what I'm saying.

PONTIUS

I'll bloody your face, Simon, if you don't shut your gob!

CARPENTER 2

I never believed the tale in the Good Book anyhow. Mary was probably some young wench knocked up by another bloke, couldn't stand to tell her husband to be—afraid he'd beat her pulpy. Any girl who can persuade the multitudes that God's the father of her bastard child—

Carpenter 1 punches Carpenter 2 in the face. They start brawling.
Enter John the Fisherman, in a loincloth.

JOHN

What's this! Ho! Hey! Stop the fighting between brothers. Stop! Haven't you heard the news? A miracle in our little town . . . you should bow your heads and be grateful.

They look down, ashamed.

A new Christ is to be born, as the Good Book prophesizes. No longer will I have to play the part of Christ. Mary is with child.

CARPENTER 2

We've heard.

JOHN

Then why all the brawling? Blood trickles down your chin, good brother.

No one speaks. Enter the Director.

DIRECTOR

What's all this? Take up your whips. We've only one week left of rehearsal—where's Mary?

JOHN

I left her home, sick with women's sickness. A glorious sickness to bear for the new Christ.

DIRECTOR

Hmmph. She'll be fined two shillings for missing rehearsal.

JOHN

You cannot fine a woman for bearing the Messiah, with all due respect, sir.

DIRECTOR

Very well. Perhaps under the circumstances. Everyone to their places. Mary, you read both parts. Pontius, let's have your speech.

PONTIUS

(As Pilate) That I am innocent of this bloode shall ye see;
Both my hands shall weshen be.

Pontius washes his hands.

DIRECTOR

Start whipping.

The chorus pretends to whip John the Fisherman.

Lamentation!

MARY 2

(As the Virgin Mary) Why? Why is my son slayn?

A tableau.

SCENE 20: JOHN AND PONTIUS

After rehearsal.

PONTIUS
You think she's God's bride, do you?

JOHN
I see God in her eyes, yes.

PONTIUS
When the baby comes out, I'll wager it'll look less like God and more like me.

JOHN
What?

PONTIUS
You heard me.

John the Fisherman looks at Pontius.
Mary's face, illuminated in a window.
A tableau.

SCENE 21: MARY AND MARY

The forest.
Mary 2 walks out and meets Mary 1.

MARY I
I hear them whispering underground, in the trees—I hear them
calling me a whore . . .

MARY 2
Don't listen. I love you, Mary. Let's run off together. I'll protect
you. We'll raise the child together as Mary and Joseph did before
us. I'll dress as a man . . . I look enough like a man . . . we'll go far
away from here.

MARY I
You don't look a bit like a man, Mary.

MARY 2
What does it matter? Then I won't dress as a man. I'll dress as
myself, but we'll go far, far away.

MARY 1

I have to leave alone, and where I'm going, no one can follow me.

MARY 2

Mary.

MARY 1

I'm a whore, Mary.

MARY 2

I would follow you anywhere, Mary.

MARY 1

No, dear. Please.
Good-bye.

Mary 1 turns to leave, but before she goes, kisses Mary 2 full on the lips.
Mary 1 leaves.
The Sky Turns Red.

MARY 2

Oh, the sky! Again, the sky!

Scene 22: The Town Square

The Village Idiot with her jack-in-the-box.

VILLAGE IDIOT

Mary not in her costume
Mary not at home.
Mary not in the lamb white days
Mary, Mary gone.

Do you know, Jack, that a woman's long hair is the last thing to float in the water? It floats, Jack, dry like a lily pad, until in one great rush it goes under—whoosh. Oh, and the fish they wept, Jack, I knew something was wrong—they cried all night and the sea bulged over the earth.

The Visiting Friar and the Director enter.

VISITING FRIAR

God has spoken with me. And God wants you to stop the Passion.

DIRECTOR

But Father, months of work . . .

VISITING FRIAR

It cannot be right, with Mary nowhere to be found. There's something strange, foreboding, in the whole business.

DIRECTOR

Which is precisely why the play must go on! We made a pact with God, when the plague had eaten the very stomach out of our village, that we would play the Passion and all for the glory of God. If we refuse, I believe that something horrible will visit our town . . . already, the sky is red.

VISITING FRIAR

But who's to play Mary?

They both look at the Village Idiot.

DIRECTOR

What do you say, dearie, would you like to take part in the play?

VILLAGE IDIOT

(Laughing, to Jack) Jack, would I like to take part in the play?
(She listens to Jack) What, Jack? I can't hear you.
(To the Director, very serious) Yes, I would like to take part in the play.

Scene 23: The Passion

A bell rings.
John the Fisherman kneels in a pool of light.
Pontius watches, in the shadows.

JOHN

Please, God, let me play the Christ well. Dear Lord, bless Mary. Please let her find her way home.

Crosses himself.

Amen.

PONTIUS

So help me God I'll kill him. I'll drive the nails in deep.

Scene 24: The Play

EVERYONE
Please lift up your hearts to behold the Holy Passion Play.

Trumpets. A tableau of the Garden of Eden.
John the Fisherman plays Adam and the Village Idiot plays Eve.
Pontius plays the snake.

JOHN
(As Adam) Ah! Eve! Thou art to blame!
On my knees I do here sink!
Against you I do exclaim
For I am naked as I think!

VILLAGE IDIOT
(As Eve) Alas, Adam, right naked so am I.
Ah, wicked worm!

She points to his privates.
Then she points to the snake.

JOHN	VILLAGE IDIOT
So that God will not see our privates and stare	So that God will not see our privates and stare
We shall cover ourselves with fig leaves	We shall cover ourselves with fig leaves
For we are naked and bare.	For we are NAKED— and all bare!

John covers himself with a fig leaf.
He then covers the Village Idiot with a fig leaf.
Suddenly, the arrival of Queen Elizabeth's courtiers, played by the Carpenters. Trumpets. Fanfare.
A murmur goes through the audience.

COURTIERS
The Queen has blessed your little town with her presence.

A louder murmur goes through the audience.
Queen Elizabeth walks onto the stage, waving.
The players bow their heads low to the ground.

THE QUEEN
My loving people.

Do you know, when they place me in my golden coffer, what they will find? They will scrape at my face with a jeweled penknife, and they will discover layer upon layer of white paint. A wall of paint as thick as this joint, in my thumb. They will be surprised. They will open their eyes wide. They do not know that Queens do not wash, and that Queens are obliged to paint their faces so that Queens do not appear to become old or ugly.

I do not want the gravediggers to scrape white paint off the dead faces of my subjects. I want my subjects to remain clean. Clean and honest and loyal to the crown. I do not want my subjects to impersonate the holy figure of Christ.

Did Christ paint his face?

No! Such things are unholy. If any man or woman in England is seen with a painted face, assuming the person of a holy figure on a stage, I will have them beheaded. Immediately.

COURTIERS
The Queen has spoken.

She turns to go. The players raise their heads slightly to watch her go. The Queen moves to exit. She stops in her tracks.

THE QUEEN
Is any house in this village concealing a priest?
My subjects should feel free to confess all of their sins to me.

No one speaks.
She walks among her people, slowing as she walks past the Visiting Friar.

HAS ANYONE IN THIS VILLAGE ANYTHING TO CONFESS?

No one speaks.

Good. I'll have my courtiers search your houses. Just to be certain.

The Queen exits with her entourage to loud fanfare.
The players are silent. They exit, one by one, collecting their props.

Scene 25: John the Fisherman's Kitchen

JOHN

Where will you go?

VISITING FRIAR

To France. Until it is safe for priests in England—when a bastard head of state is severed from its body.

JOHN

I don't understand you, good Friar.

VISITING FRIAR

Good. When they come, asking questions, you can say truly: I've no idea. I only made the man some eggs. Do you have anything to confess before I go?

JOHN

Perhaps there is something. I believe I liked it a little too well, playing the role of Christ.

VISITING FRIAR

God be with you.

JOHN

And with you.

Scene 26: The Town Square

*The Director, Carpenter 1, Carpenter 2, Pontius, Mary 2, the Machinist
and the Village Idiot.*
One by one, the players hand in their costumes to the Director.
They are sad.
The Machinist hands in his emperor costume.

DIRECTOR
We can get five shillings for this. No, seven—that's fine material,
good stitching.

Mary 2 hands in her costume.

Eight for this.

Mary 2 holds Mary 1's halo.

MARY 2
May I keep this?

DIRECTOR

I'll wager the professional acting companies in London have no
need for halos. Keep it. Only hide it.

Carpenter 1 hands in his angel wings.

This one's damaged.

CARPENTER I

From flying.

DIRECTOR

Throw it out.

Suddenly, John the Fisherman enters with the body of Mary 1.
She is dripping wet.
Water pours out of her mouth onto the stage.
Water continues to pour out of her and off of her.
Everyone turns to look in horror.

JOHN

I fished her out of the sea—

John lays the body down.
A tableau.

Scene 27: The Death of Pontius

The sky is red.
Pontius, by the body of Mary 1, holds a knife.
John the Fisherman is fishing on the other side of the stage,
as if in a dream.

PONTIUS

No more bloody play, Mary.
You needn't have drowned yourself, dear.
My cousin is beside himself. He's out in the boat fishing.
The fish drink up his salty tears.

The moon is cradled by the night—the curved white slipper of the
moon, reclining, rocked back into the night, will rock me to sleep.
Mary, the doctor who birthed me, see, he didn't sew up my belly
properly. My belly is an open wound and the air—she smites it.
There is nothing left for me, Mary, but to find you. I will swim to
you, arms outstretched.

So that no man in the world may
Give me a cruel death;

My own heart
With my knife I will pierce—
Oh, alas, and welaway—

*He stabs himself with a knife. He closes his eyes. Drums. Big beautiful
fish puppets surround him, lift him up, and carry him offstage. The sky
turns blue.*

Intermission.

PASSION PLAY

PART TWO

Oberammergau, Bavaria, 1934

◆

CHARACTERS

FOOT SOLDIER	plays Pontius Pilate (was Ponitus the Fish Gutter in Part One)
ERIC	plays Jesus (was John the Fisherman in Part One)
ELSA	plays the Virgin Mary (was Mary 1 in Part One)
MARY 2	plays Mary Magdalen; Eric's sister (was Mary 2 in Part One)
VISITING ENGLISHMAN OR SIMON LILY	(was Visiting Friar in Part One)
VIOLET	dressed as a normal girl (was Village Idiot in Part One)
CARPENTER 1 OR JOHANN	also plays ensemble roles and bird (was Carpenter 1 in Part One).
CARPENTER 2 OR LUDWIG	also plays ensemble roles (was Carpenter 2 in Part One)
DIRECTOR OR ROCHUS SCHALLHAMMER	(was Director in Part One)
GERMAN OFFICER	(was Machinist in Part One)
HITLER	(was Queen Elizabeth in Part One)

SET

The suggestion of a forest.
A playing space.

Scene 1: Prologue

CHORUS

Oberammergau, 1934!
The Passion Play's three-hundred-year anniversary.

Special Passion Play trains—
One-third the usual cost!

Visit the Oberammergau Carving Shop.
Crucifixes of every style. Made to Order.
Cheapest Prices. Good Service.

Visit our biggest hotel. Exceptionally hygienic.
Near the woods and free from dust.
Price, out of Passion season, 4 marks.
Price, during Passion season, 12 marks.

The sound of a train whistle.

SCENE 2

The Visiting Englishman is writing a letter.
Violet sits nearby, playing with a white ribbon.

VISITING ENGLISHMAN

Second of April, 1934.

Dearest Harriet,

Oberammergau is certainly quaint. A more friendly and peaceful place could hardly be found in Europe. There is, of course, quite a lot of Catholic superstition here—they certainly do not have a very complex understanding of the relation between art and life. Today, as I wandered through the town square, I saw the most remarkable little girl crying slow, medieval tears.

"What's the matter?" I asked.

The Visiting Englishman leaves off his letter-writing to enact the scene.

VIOLET

I haven't a part. A part in the play. I would so love to be in the play.
But only the natives of Oberammergau have parts.

VISITING ENGLISHMAN

That doesn't seem fair.

VIOLET

Fair's fair. I am an outsider and haven't the look of an Oberammergauer.

VISITING ENGLISHMAN

And what is the look of the Oberammergauer?

VIOLET

To be jolly and fat.

VISITING ENGLISHMAN

And you are not so very jolly.

VIOLET

No.

VISITING ENGLISHMAN

And what's your name, my dear?

VIOLET

They call me the village idiot.

VISITING ENGLISHMAN

Surely that's not your name?

VIOLET

No. My name means Violet in another language. The children here
can't pronounce it. So they call me the village idiot.

VISITING ENGLISHMAN

Don't your parents get very upset when nasty children call you names?

VIOLET

My parents are gone.

VISITING ENGLISHMAN

Ah, I see. Well. *I* shall call you Violet. So, tell me, Violet, why do you play with that little white ribbon?

VIOLET

It is pretty, I suppose, and naughty too.

VISITING ENGLISHMAN

Why naughty?

VIOLET

Like the white drool of a snake.

VISITING ENGLISHMAN

Mmm, yes, quite.

VIOLET

Why do you say yes when you don't know what you mean. You don't know about the white drool of a snake. I made it up. I'm going to take the white ribbon with me.

VISITING ENGLISHMAN

Are you running away, dearie?

VIOLET

I might.

VISITING ENGLISHMAN

Whatever for?

VIOLET

The people here give me a funny feeling. I've been making the sky turn red but no one notices.

VISITING ENGLISHMAN

Perhaps the sun makes the sky turn red.

VIOLET

At two in the afternoon?
Do you know the story of Little Red Riding Hood?

VISITING ENGLISHMAN

Yes.

VIOLET

Will you tell it to me?

VISITING ENGLISHMAN

Once upon a time, there was a little girl. Her grandmother was sick, so the little girl went to bring her a basket of goodies. Then a big bad wolf came along. And the little girl was afraid.

VIOLET

Yes, she was very afraid.

VISITING ENGLISHMAN

The wolf howled and bared his teeth. But, as it turns out, the girl and the wolf got along just fine. They became good friends, and lived happily ever after.

VIOLET

Did they?

VISITING ENGLISHMAN

Well, yes, of course they did.

VIOLET

Oh. When I run away to the forest, I will keep my white ribbon with me at all times.

VISITING ENGLISHMAN

Perhaps you should take bread crumbs.

VIOLET

No—bread crumbs are unreliable. Bread crumbs are eaten by birds.

Scene 3

Eric is on the cross. The Carpenters measure him.

CARPENTER 2

Steady, now, hands out, that's right. Never understood how a man could stomach playing Jesus. Couldn't have any fun. No rolls in the hay, huh?

ERIC

No.

CARPENTER 2

Couldn't even fart in church. I'd be shy of farting in my own home, come to think of it, were I playing the Christus.

CARPENTER 1

Hard to imagine you shy of fa-farting in your own home, Ludwig.

CARPENTER 2

Well, and you too, you randy old bastard.

CARPENTER I

Th-that's enough, Ludwig.

CARPENTER 2

No one lets me have fun anymore. Not even my own brother. Big
Director Man's getting a puffed-up serious head like a ripe tomato.
A new Germany and all that. Playing your part, however small.
Once upon a time we played jokes—there was the year we made big
wooden testicles and shoved them between the legs of old Fritz
when he played the Christ.
(He laughs a little too long) Those were the days—the days when a
man laughed at a good joke. Now everyone's a poker-faced pansy
trying to make a buck and look holier than the next guy.

(To Eric) What's wrong? Cat got your tongue?

ERIC

I'm sorry—I'm trying to memorize my lines.

CARPENTER 2

Still don't have 'em down, after watching your father do the Christus for twenty years?

ERIC

I never thought I'd have the role, to be honest.

CARPENTER I

The Ch-Christus must stay in the f-family.

CARPENTER 2

How'd your father take the news?

ERIC

He's ill.

CARPENTER I

B-best man that ever b-breathed.

ERIC

Yes.

CARPENTER 2

He couldn't do it forever. A white-haired Christus can't stay on the cross for five hours, rehearsing. D'you know what happened to the real Christ when they put him on that cross? First the wrists rip under the weight of the nails, then the shoulders and elbows dislocate. The lungs go kaput, the organs dry out, and it's a miracle He can talk at all. Probably died of a heart attack. Bet you didn't know that, didja?

ERIC

No.

CARPENTER 2

You're big on the one-syllable words today, huh?

ERIC

I'm sorry—I'm trying to memorize my lines.

CARPENTER 2

Don't worry, I'm done talking. Your measurements, my good man, have been taken.

Scene 4

Eric and the Foot Soldier. Day.

ERIC

When will you leave? Do they tell you?

FOOT SOLDIER

Soon.

ERIC

Won't you be homesick?

FOOT SOLDIER

I'll have the whole world to entertain me.

ERIC

And you'll leave even if it means not playing Pontius Pilate?

FOOT SOLDIER

Plays aren't real. The soldier's boot—that's real.

ERIC

I should like to come with you.

FOOT SOLDIER

The Christus cannot come with the soldier. The Christus must stay behind.

ERIC

I'm tired of crucifixions.

FOOT SOLDIER

You are?

ERIC

My arms are tired. I was on the cross for four hours yesterday, rehearsing. I tried to raise a cup of water to my mouth and couldn't, I was shaking so badly.

FOOT SOLDIER

I could rub them.

ERIC

All right.

The Foot Soldier rubs Eric's arms.

FOOT SOLDIER

Let's play a game. It's called would you rather.

ERIC

All right.

FOOT SOLDIER

Would you rather be a just beggar or an unjust king?

ERIC

A just beggar. The pangs of conscience are worse than the pangs of hunger.

FOOT SOLDIER

I should have known you were one of those.

ERIC

Well, what would you rather?

FOOT SOLDIER

An unjust king, of course. The pangs of conscience are barely audible when the stomach is growling. Would you rather be a dwarf or a hermaphrodite?

ERIC

A dwarf, I suppose.

FOOT SOLDIER

For all the world to see your shame?

ERIC

My turn. Would you rather be a mediocre composer whose name was remembered for centuries, or a glorious composer lost to obscurity?

FOOT SOLDIER

A glorious composer lost to obscurity, of course. You?

ERIC

The same! Would you rather be Christ or Pontius Pilate?

FOOT SOLDIER

Pontius Pilate.

ERIC

Why?

FOOT SOLDIER

Very unpleasant, the nails, the whipping, the blood . . . No one actually wants to *be* Christ, they only want to admire him from a distance.

ERIC

That's not a very nice thing to say.

FOOT SOLDIER

But it's true. My turn. Would you rather be me or you?

ERIC

That's a strange question.

FOOT SOLDIER

Go on.

ERIC

Let's see . . . if I were you I would take everything as a joke—I would get drunk to forget my troubles and I would have the most interesting, intelligent eyes. No one would know me but everyone would like me. If I were me, I would be—timid. I would take little bites of food and fall in love with the wrong people.

FOOT SOLDIER

You still haven't answered the question.

ERIC

I would rather be you in the evening and I would rather be me in the morning.

FOOT SOLDIER

Why?

ERIC

I could soak myself with pleasure in the evening and not remember in the morning. And you—would you rather be me or you?

FOOT SOLDIER

I would rather be me in wartime and you in peacetime.

ERIC

Why is that?

FOOT SOLDIER

I couldn't carry a gun properly if I had your little hands.

ERIC

Little! I don't have little hands—

He holds his hands up to the Foot Soldier's hands.

FOOT SOLDIER

You know what they say about the size of a man's hands.

ERIC

No.

FOOT SOLDIER

Think about it. If you have big hands, maybe other things will be big.

Eric takes his hands away.

ERIC

Gloves?

FOOT SOLDIER

Don't act stupid. You know what I'm talking about.

ERIC

You have a perverse imagination.

FOOT SOLDIER

We could compare. It's important to know these things.

ERIC

I have rehearsal.

FOOT SOLDIER

Not for another hour.

ERIC

I don't know my lines.

FOOT SOLDIER

All right, all right, I'll stop bothering you. You want a cigarette?

ERIC

Okay.

The Foot Soldier gives Eric a cigarette.
Eric puffs on it without sophistication.

FOOT SOLDIER

Here—hold it like this—that's better. That's how they hold cigarettes in Berlin.

ERIC

How would you know?

FOOT SOLDIER

I've seen pictures.

ERIC

I have to memorize my lines.

FOOT SOLDIER

Should I test you?

ERIC

Okay.

FOOT SOLDIER

Art thou the King of the Jews?

Pause. Eric doesn't remember his line.

Art thou the King of the Jews?

ERIC

Ahh . . . Dost thou say this of thine own accord—or—or—

FOOT SOLDIER

(Giving him the line) Or—have—others . . .

ERIC

said it of me?

FOOT SOLDIER

Good.

(Performing) Am I a Jew? Thine own people handed thee over to me. They say that thou wouldst make thyself King of the Jews.

ERIC

My kingdom is of—

FOOT SOLDIER

Not—

ERIC

My kingdom is *not* of this world.

FOOT SOLDIER

Thou art a king then!

ERIC

Thou sayest so.

FOOT SOLDIER

What is the truth?

Pause.

ERIC

I'm sorry. I can't concentrate. Every time I say my lines I think of my father watching me and my mind goes blank.

FOOT SOLDIER

Your father was an old man playing the Christ. You're a young man.
You need to play *that* Christ—a leader of men—a leader of nations—

ERIC

I'd rather play Judas. To be hated, that's easy. To be loved—that's
hard.

FOOT SOLDIER

You need to relax. Have more fun. We'll go mushroom hunting this
afternoon.

ERIC

I should sit with my father—he's been getting worse.

FOOT SOLDIER

Come on. A nice tender mushroom . . . picked with your own
hands . . .

ERIC

Well—all right. I shouldn't let you go all by yourself. You're a horrible judge of mushrooms.

SCENE 5

The Visiting Englishman interviews Mary 2, outside her father's sickroom.

VISITING ENGLISHMAN

I have once heard it said that one can measure the degree to which a village is civilized by the variety of fungi it eats.

MARY 2

Oberammergau has all kinds of mushrooms.

VISITING ENGLISHMAN

Does it?

MARY 2

Oh, yes! Only you have to be careful. Some mushrooms, when broken apart, spread through and through with beautiful reds and unearthly greens. But secretly, they're poisonous.

VISITING ENGLISHMAN

Are they deadly?

MARY 2

Oh, yes.

VISITING ENGLISHMAN

I suppose I'd better stay out of the forest then.

MARY 2

Oh—but Oberammergau has the most beautiful forests in Bavaria!

VISITING ENGLISHMAN

Well, then, perhaps I'd better take my jaunts in the forest but defer to the native's superior judgment in the art of distinguishing between mushrooms. *(He laughs)*

MARY 2

(She does not laugh) That's a good idea.
Why have you come to our town?

VISITING ENGLISHMAN

Actually, I'm writing a book on the theater.

MARY 2

Really? A whole book!

VISITING ENGLISHMAN

Well, yes. Do you mind if I ask you some questions?

MARY 2

Please.

VISITING ENGLISHMAN

Is it true that your father plays the role of Christ in the Passion?

MARY 2

Not this year. Father is too old, so they gave the part to my brother, which is, of course, a great honor.

VISITING ENGLISHMAN
Was your father disappointed when he heard the news?

MARY 2
Oh, yes. He took ill the very next day.

VISITING ENGLISHMAN
And how did you feel, as a little girl, watching your father play the Christus?

MARY 2
I hated to see his side pierced and the blood running out. I confess I had to stop myself from crying out. I wanted with all my heart to run onstage and fight the Jews. I could not understand why all the people watching did nothing.

VISITING ENGLISHMAN
Your father has quite a reputation as a holy man.

MARY 2
Oh, yes. When father and I walked together through the forests, Christ would walk with us.

VISITING ENGLISHMAN
Right.

MARY 2
Father had many offers from America to come play parts in New York City. But he preferred to stay here.

VISITING ENGLISHMAN
I'm afraid your father's genius would be lost on Americans. The only art Americans understand is the big red painting that matches the big red rug on their living room floor.

He laughs.

MARY 2

I don't know—I'm afraid I've never been to America. If you'll excuse me, I should give Father his supper.

VISITING ENGLISHMAN

May I take his picture before I go?

MARY 2

I'm sorry, but Papa doesn't pose for pictures.

Scene 6: A Rehearsal

The Visiting Englishman takes pictures.
Eric rushes in late.

DIRECTOR

CHRIST TEARS DOWN THE TEMPLE! Begin!

ERIC

What—what do I see here? Is this God's house? Or is it naught but—naught to you but—

MARY 2

What is wrong with you?

ERIC

(Whispering to Mary 2) I can't remember my lines . . .

MARY 2

You were supposed to practice them this afternoon! Where were you?

ERIC

In the forest—

DIRECTOR

(To Eric, giving lines) Or is it naught to you but a marketplace?

ERIC

Or is it naught to you but a marketplace? You dishonor the abode of my father. You—money-changers—

Violet enacts her own play to compete with the other play, which she doesn't like.

VIOLET

I don't like that story.
How about—once upon a time there
were children named Hansel
and Gretel.

DIRECTOR

Shut up, village idiot. Jewish chorus, your lines!

JEWISH CHORUS

My money, ah, my money! Who will restore this loss to me?

DIRECTOR

(To Eric) Push the vessel this time! Again!

Eric pushes over a vessel of money and the Jewish chorus picks up the gold coins.

VIOLET

Hansel and Gretel ate delicious
candies off an old witch's house.

JEWISH CHORUS

My money, ah, my money!

DIRECTOR

Release the doves!

Eric opens a bird cage and two doves fly out.

JEWISH CHORUS

My doves!

VIOLET

The birds ate up
their bread crumbs.
When people are chasing
you through the forest,
Don't rely on bread crumbs.

ERIC

Away from here, Servants of Mammon! I bid you go! Take what is
yours, and leave this holy place!

CARPENTER I

(As Jewish Chorus) What b-boastful insolent talk!

DIRECTOR

Again. Try not to stutter this time.

CARPENTER I

(As Jewish Chorus) What b-boastful insolent talk.

DIRECTOR

See me privately after rehearsal, Johann. We need to discuss the
renewal of your contract.

CARPENTER I

Yes, sir.

VIOLET

Then the old witch wanted to fatten Hansel up—
but Hansel was smart to put a

little bone outside of his
cage to look like a finger—

DIRECTOR

I said, shut your mouth village idiot! Continue!

ERIC

Do not destroy this temple—
No—Destroy this temple—

VIOLET

One day, the witch got
hungry and said, Hansel,
I'm going to cook you in
the oven!

DIRECTOR

Your lines!
Destroy this temple, and in three days
I will raise it up again!

VIOLET

(To Eric) Hansel was scared.
Wouldn't you be scared?
If someone wanted to push
you in an oven?

ERIC

Destroy this temple, and I
will, I will—

VIOLET

But then Hansel pushed
the *witch* into the oven.
He said, with your fat bottom,
you'd make a better dinner!

DIRECTOR

I said, shut your mouth, village idiot!

VIOLET

And the witch screamed
from inside the oven, like
this, AAAAAAAAAAH!

DIRECTOR

(Moving to Violet) The only people who should be speaking in this rehearsal are the people with parts in the play. Do you have a part in this play?

VIOLET

No, sir.

DIRECTOR

Then I suggest you practice being silent. Do you know how to be silent?

Violet opens her mouth to speak.

Don't answer me—only nod.

Violet nods.

Good. Because if children do not learn how to be silent, the world will teach them. Do you understand? Don't answer me—only nod.

She nods.

Let's move on to the Jewish High Council, Scene 3. Caiaphas, you stand here. Take it from: "All moves excellently well, worthy Fathers."

CARPENTER 2

(As Caiaphas) All moves excellently well, worthy Fathers. Now: what shall we do with this Jesus of Nazareth, once He is delivered into our hands?

CARPENTER 1

(As Rabbi) Let Him be thrown into the deepest, darkest dungeon, and kept there! Let Him go through a living death!

DIRECTOR

Very good, Johann.

CARPENTER 2

(As Caiaphas) No. He must die! Until He dies there is no peace in Israel, no safety for the Law of Moses!

DIRECTOR

Try your lower register for the first line, and work your way up to the end of the speech.

CARPENTER 2

(Better acting) No. He must die! Until He dies there is no peace in Israel, no safety for the Law of Moses!

DIRECTOR

Yes—I think that'll work.

SCENE 7

Elsa alone in her dressing room, looking in the mirror.
Enter the German Officer. Her face changes.

GERMAN OFFICER

You were a very pretty picture at rehearsal. Were those real tears?

ELSA

An actress doesn't give away her secrets.

GERMAN OFFICER

You are very cruel. Would you wash my feet, Elsa, the way you wash the feet of Christ?

ELSA

Your feet might smell from being stuck in those big black boots all day.

GERMAN OFFICER

You're like a sphinx, Elsa. You should be in the moving pictures.

ELSA

Please, sir.

GERMAN OFFICER

I have a very pretty house, in a very pretty forest, with very pretty pewter mugs. I have a lamp shade from the Kaiser himself. I fly small, fast planes all over the world. But upon my return, there is no one to sit at my table and smile sweetly.

ELSA

Lamp shades don't make for very good company.

GERMAN OFFICER

They say that the Marys of Oberammergau do not marry because they want to keep their parts. I hope you are not one of the foolish ones, Elsa.

ELSA

Do I look foolish?

GERMAN OFFICER

No.

ELSA

I have now refused three men all for the dream of playing Mary. All of them now settled into clean little homes with clean little wives, not half so pretty as I am.

There is an old saying about a woman who goes searching for sticks in the forest. She passes by many sticks because she wants to find the straightest one. By the time she reaches the edge of the forest, only crooked sticks are left. Do you understand me?

GERMAN OFFICER

A smile like that would make any man want to *misunderstand* you.

He moves in to kiss her. She stops him.

ELSA

A man who has the milk for free will not buy the cow, sir.

GERMAN OFFICER

You speak of sticks and cows. I am a blunt man, Elsa. Will you ever marry?

ELSA

Is that a proposal, sir?

GERMAN OFFICER

Is that a yes?

ELSA

I wish to play Mary one last time. And after—

GERMAN OFFICER

After?

ELSA

Perhaps—

GERMAN OFFICER

A man cannot live on perhaps.

ELSA

But there are many kinds of perhaps—perhaps you *can* live on perhaps—

GERMAN OFFICER

Perhaps like this?

He slides his hand up her dress.

ELSA

Perhaps—

He slides his hand further.
She smiles.

But no one must know—

GERMAN OFFICER

Oh, Elsa.

She puts a finger to her lips.
He grabs her.

Scene 8: Night

Mary 2 and Eric at home. Eric is reading a book.

MARY 2

What are you reading?

ERIC

Nothing.

She snatches his book—a volume of Rilke.

MARY 2

Oooh—poetry! Since when do you like poetry? Rose, oh pure contradiction, joy of being . . .

ERIC

Don't! Put it down.

She puts the book down.

MARY 2

Sorry. Who gave it to you? The foot soldier?

ERIC

None of your business.

MARY 2

Do you like it?

ERIC

Yes I like it.

MARY 2

Well, I've never understood poetry.

ERIC

Your loss.

MARY 2

I often think that people who write books are stupid, solitary people. They begin as sickly children, with no friends, so they make
books into friends. But they don't write books to befriend lonely
children—no—out of their bitterness they write books to make
men lonely.

ERIC

I want to leave, Mary.

MARY 2

What?

ERIC

I want to leave . . . I want to join something . . . bigger than myself
. . . bigger than this town . . . I always thought I wanted to play the
Christus. Well, I don't believe in plays anymore. The soldier's
boot—that's real. The life of the soldier—there's something.

MARY 2

You should be honored to play your part. Father is dying, all for the loss of the Christus, and you spouting this!

ERIC

I want to see the world.

MARY 2

This isn't the world?

ERIC

No, this isn't the world! I want to see steam engines and skyscrapers and great big opera houses.

MARY 2

You want to see the underpants of French dancers!

ERIC

Things are happening in the world, Mary. Exciting things. They're building a new Germany—there's hope for the future and jobs for everyone—

MARY 2

You have a job.

ERIC

Carving crucifixes for tourists all day? That's not a job for a man.

MARY 2

And what would you fight for? What did Father fight for? He came back to a dead country with no gold left in its pockets. You should spend more time with Father and less time dreaming of wars that are never going to happen!

ERIC

Let's not fight, Mary.

A silence.

MARY 2

Do you remember when we were little—you stayed home sick from
school one day. You were supposed to feed my bird. I said, no matter what, don't let my bird fly outside. You played with the bird. It
flew like crazy around the kitchen. You were afraid the bird would
fly into the garden so you slammed the kitchen door as the bird was
flying out and you killed it. I came home from school and you had
the strangest look on your face. What's wrong? I said. Nothing, you
said. Then all of a sudden you started crying. I killed your bird, you
said. And now no one will ever love me.

ERIC

I remember.

MARY 2

How could a boy like that join the army?

Scene 9: The Visiting Englishman and the Director

The Director comes upon the Visiting Englishman, who is startled.

DIRECTOR
I don't know you.

VISITING ENGLISHMAN
I don't suppose we've been introduced, then, have we?

DIRECTOR
No.

VISITING ENGLISHMAN
Simon Lily.

DIRECTOR
Rochus Schallhammer.

VISITING ENGLISHMAN
Ah! The director of the Passion. Delighted.

The Visiting Englishman extends his hand. The Director shakes it, firmly.

DIRECTOR

What brings you to our town?

VISITING ENGLISHMAN

Well, actually, I'm writing a book on the theater.

DIRECTOR

Really. A whole book!

VISITING ENGLISHMAN

Why, yes.

DIRECTOR

Maybe you should ask me some questions. An interview. For the book. You know.

VISITING ENGLISHMAN

Well, let's see. I'm quite unprepared, you know. Umm . . . right. Do you *enjoy* directing the Passion?

DIRECTOR

Yes. I enjoy.

VISITING ENGLISHMAN

Right. Good. Umm . . . *Why* do you enjoy directing the Passion?

DIRECTOR

I will confess something to you. There are times in every man's life—in his personal life even—when he needs a director. His eyes are muddy. Maybe he has a sty. Maybe his hands are tied. Whatever it is—he can't see—he can't think. He needs someone with vision—me—someone stronger—me—to tell him what to do.

VISITING ENGLISHMAN

Ah, I see. How marvelous.

DIRECTOR

Why don't you write down?

VISITING ENGLISHMAN

Oh, how stupid of me, really. Do you mind repeating yourself?

DIRECTOR

No. I don't mind. There are times in every man's life—in his personal life even—when he needs a director. His eyes are muddy. Maybe he has a sty. Maybe his hands are tied. Whatever it is—he can't see—he can't think. He needs someone with vision—me—someone stronger—me—to tell him what to do.

VISITING ENGLISHMAN

To tell him what to do . . . there. I believe I've got the whole speech down, Herr Schallhammer. Thank you very much indeed.

DIRECTOR

Not at all. I like to help.

SCENE 10: THE LAST SUPPER — A REHEARSAL

Violet hides under the Last Supper table. The cast moves into the Last Supper tableau. Eric rushes into place, late.

DIRECTOR

Places, places for the Last Supper!
(To Eric) You're late!

MARY 2

(Whispering) Where were you?

ERIC

Mushroom hunting.

MARY 2

Honestly!

VISITING ENGLISHMAN

(To Eric) May I take your photograph?

ERIC

I'd better not—they sell them at the tourist bureau—

The bulb flashes.

VISITING ENGLISHMAN

Oops!

DIRECTOR

(To Eric) Your lines!

ERIC

(Whispering urgently to Mary 2) Mary, I can't remember my lines . . .

MARY 2

What's wrong with you?

VIOLET

(Whispering to him from under the table) I have longed to share this Passover with you before I suffer.

The Director busies himself fixing the tableau.

ERIC

(Loud and performative) I have longed to share this Passover with you before I suffer.
(Whispering to Violet) Thank you! Do you know the next bit?

VIOLET

Verily, verily, I say unto you, one of you at this table will betray me.

ERIC

(To Violet) Yes—that's it! Clever girl!
Verily, verily, I say unto you, one of you at this table will betray me.

DISCIPLES

What! A betrayer amongst us? Impossible!

Eric turns to Violet to see if she knows the next line.
She feeds him the lines.

VIOLET	ERIC *(Echoing)*
I *will* forgive sinners	I *will* forgive sinners
but it's probably best not to sin	but it's probably best not to sin
in the first place.	in the first place.
You have to admit, some	You have to admit, some
pretty strange things will	pretty strange things will
be done in my name.	be done in my name.
In time,	In time,
you will crawl around like	you will crawl around like
pigs snorting in the mud	pigs snorting in the mud
looking for the answer to	looking for the answer to
this fundamental question:	this fundamental question:
is there a God?	is there a God?

Eric works himself up into a performative lather.

And if you decide that there	And if you decide that there
is no God, will you need	is no God, will you need
someone with vision,	someone with vision,
someone stronger,	someone stronger,
to tell you what to do?	to tell you what to do?
Resist,	Resist,
I say unto you!	I say unto you!
	(Becoming almost simultaneous)
And finally, I want everyone	And finally, I want everyone
at this table,	at this table,
eating my blood and my body,	eating my blood and my body,
to remember that	to remember that
I am a Jew.	I am a Jew.
Wait. This is not—	

DIRECTOR

What is that voice?

GERMAN OFFICER

The Village Idiot.

The Director pulls Violet out from under the table.

DIRECTOR

I propose that the village idiot be put in this box with no food for one week as punishment for mocking the voice of Christ. All in favor say aye.

ALL

(With the exception of the Visiting Englishman) AYE.

The Visiting Englishman flashes a picture.
The Director puts Violet in the empty bird-cage prop.

VIOLET

If you lock me up, I'll make the sky turn red. Now, now!

She closes her eyes. The sky remains the same.

Did you see that? Did you see?

No one sees.

SCENE 11

Mary 2 and Eric.

MARY 2

How could you forget your lines?

ERIC

I was confused.

MARY 2

You were more than confused! You were stupid. Father says you should pray more. He says if you feel the grace of God, you'll remember the right words.

ERIC

Father says this, Father says that. Why don't you find yourself a husband to boss around.

I'm sorry.

MARY 2

What is *wrong* with you lately?

ERIC

Mary. I've been thinking. When Father played his part, he got this—
funny glow on his face, do you remember? Sort of like this . . .

He demonstrates.

I've been trying to get a glow on my face when I say my part.

MARY 2

Most of the people in the audience will see you from a distance.
They will not be able to tell if your face is glowing.

ERIC

I know—but—

MARY 2

And the people in the front row—they paid a lot of *money* to see
your face glow—so they will *imagine* that your face is glowing,
even if it's not. The important thing is to remember your lines. And
to say them. Word for word.

ERIC

But, there's a difference, isn't there? When you do—a thing—and
feel—a thing—at the same time?

MARY 2

I don't understand.

ERIC

I mean—when you're playing your part—or other times—have
you ever felt—the grace of God pour into you like a fever? So you
don't have to—decide—I think this or I think that—suddenly
you're bigger than yourself—and you're looking at the clouds—
isn't that how it's supposed to feel?

MARY 2

How *what's* supposed to feel?

ERIC

Anything—big—important—love—or—or—art—or marching
with hundreds of people—

MARY 2

Are you in love?

ERIC

No!

A pause.

Wait. Did you hear that?

There was no sound.

MARY 2

What is it?

ERIC

Go—look in his room—

MARY 2

You.

ERIC

You.

MARY 2

You.

ERIC

No.

MARY 2

Why?

ERIC

I'm afraid.

MARY 2

There's nothing to be afraid of.

ERIC

Then hurry.

She looks in their father's room.

Is he breathing?

MARY 2

I don't think so.

ERIC

My God.
We have to call a doctor.

MARY 2

What for?

ERIC

But his body . . .

MARY 2

(With compassion) Go see. It's nothing to be frightened of. It's a body. That's all.

Scene 12

Violet in her box.

VIOLET

A cross is like someone is cross with you so he folds his arms across his chest. A cross is like I cross my heart and hope to die—is like telling the truth, the whole truth and nothing but the truth. A cross is like I'm cross-eyed so I can't see.

Eric enters. He removes his shoes and socks.
He goes to the stage, walking through his blocking. She watches him.

Hello.

ERIC

You startled me.

VIOLET

You look sad.

ERIC

I—never mind.

VIOLET

What are you doing?

ERIC

Rehearsing.

VIOLET

In the middle of the night? Which part?

ERIC

It's called The Mount of Olives.

VIOLET

What happens in that part?

ERIC

I ask my disciples to watch with me for an hour. But they fall asleep.

VIOLET

Why?

ERIC

They're tired.

VIOLET

Oh. That sounds like a nice part. I get tired of the bloody parts. I wish there were more miracle parts—making five hundred fish out of one fish. Or walking on water.

ERIC

I suppose it's hard to put onstage—walking on water.

VIOLET

No, they could do it. People like the bloody parts better.

ERIC

Yes, I suppose they do.

You tricked me at rehearsal, didn't you?

VIOLET

I only meant to help.

ERIC

Did you?

VIOLET

Yes.

ERIC

Do you want to get out of that box?

VIOLET

Yes.

Eric lets her out of the box.

Thank you.

ERIC

Now run along and don't tell anyone. Go on now. Good night.

She runs offstage.
He remains, in the night.
A large orange moon appears in the sky. Eric looks at the moon.
The German Officer enters and looks on, unobserved.
The Foot Soldier comes behind Eric, putting his hands over Eric's eyes.

FOOT SOLDIER

What do you see?

ERIC

The moon is huge—orange and bloody—a laughing judge—pre-siding over an orange trial.

The Foot Soldier takes his hands away.

                                    FOOT SOLDIER
Now look. The moon is gold.

                                        ERIC
I'm afraid.

                                    FOOT SOLDIER
What are you afraid of, little Christ?

                                        ERIC
Everything.

                                    FOOT SOLDIER
Perhaps we should switch roles. I don't want to put you to death.

                                        ERIC
But you have to.

                                    FOOT SOLDIER
What if I refused? What if I saved you from the mob—took you
home with me, bathed your wounds with warm water?

                                        ERIC
Impossible.

                                    FOOT SOLDIER
Why impossible? You see only the mountain, you must learn to see
the sky on the other side.

                                        ERIC
The foot soldier is a dreamer.

                                    FOOT SOLDIER
The Christus has no faith.

They embrace.
The German Officer looks on, unobserved.

Scene 13

Day. Backstage. The German Officer, Elsa and the Foot Soldier. Elsa arranges her halo in an imaginary mirror.

GERMAN OFFICER

Oh, Elsa, you look exquisite.

He touches her.

(To the Foot Soldier) Doesn't she?
What do you say, soldier? Cat got your tongue?

FOOT SOLDIER

Yes, sir.

GERMAN OFFICER

The foot soldier does not appreciate women as I do. Soldier, come here!

FOOT SOLDIER

Yes, sir.

GERMAN OFFICER

Place your hand on the Virgin's behind.

FOOT SOLDIER

I'd rather not, sir.

GERMAN OFFICER

It's an order.

The Foot Soldier places his hand on Elsa's behind.

This, soldier, in your hands, is womanly flesh. It feels something like a melon, or a ripe squash. Ripe, deliciously ripe, almost falling from the branch, but not quite fallen. That's what makes it so tantalizing. Understand?

FOOT SOLDIER

Yes, sir.

GERMAN OFFICER

I want you to remember. Repeat after me. This is a woman's flesh.

FOOT SOLDIER

This is a woman's flesh.

GERMAN OFFICER

It feels something like a melon, or a ripe squash.

FOOT SOLDIER

It feels something like a melon, or a ripe squash.

GERMAN OFFICER

How I love womanly flesh.

FOOT SOLDIER

How I love womanly flesh.

GERMAN OFFICER

Soldier, do you know what happens to men in the German army who do not appreciate women the way a man should?

FOOT SOLDIER

I don't know what you mean, sir.

GERMAN OFFICER

Oh, I think you do.

Enter the Visiting Englishman.

VISITING ENGLISHMAN

Knock, knock . . . Am I interrupting something?

GERMAN OFFICER

No.

VISITING ENGLISHMAN

Well, I suppose everyone's nervous about opening night—got the jitters as they say. I must say, I'm bursting with excitement. You're looking lovely, Elsa.

ELSA

Thank you.

VISITING ENGLISHMAN

Well. I suppose you have to put on your makeup and what not?

ELSA

We don't wear makeup, Mr. Lily.

VISITING ENGLISHMAN

Really! I could have sworn you had rouge on your cheeks.

ELSA

Here—come see if you like.

The Visiting Englishman goes to her. He tries to rub the rouge off her cheeks. There is none.

VISITING ENGLISHMAN

Remarkable.

ELSA

You see, here in Oberammergau, everything is as it appears to be.

A bell rings, ushering the audience into the theater.

SCENE 14

Eric prays in a pool of light.

ERIC

Dear God, let me play Christ well for the sake of my father. I know I am unworthy of the part. Please forgive my sins—I won't name them—you know them all.

Enter the Director.

DIRECTOR

Get up. Places.

ERIC

Yes, sir.

DIRECTOR

Don't forget your lines today.

ERIC

I won't, sir.

DIRECTOR

Because, if you do, you'll disgrace not only me, but your father,
your faith, your village, and your nation. Do you understand me?

ERIC

Yes.

DIRECTOR

Good.

The Director leaves. Eric rehearses to himself, softly.
Mary 2 enters quietly and watches.

ERIC

Many shall come in my name, saying "I am Christ" and shall
deceive the multitudes . . . For false Christs and false prophets shall
rise. The sun shall be darkened, and the moon shall not give her
light . . . Take heed. Watch and pray; lest coming suddenly He find
you sleeping. And this is what I say unto all: watch.

MARY 2

You remembered your lines.

They embrace.

Scene 15

Curtains are pulled back to reveal Pontius Pilate and an angry crowd.
They strike a tableau for a moment.

PILATE

Listen, men of Judea! Behold these two—one with gentle countenance, the other a convicted robber and murderer—

CROWD

Free Barabas!

PILATE

I appeal to your human sympathy. Here is Jesus of Nazareth—of
worthy bearing—

CROWD

Crucify him! Crucify him!

PILATE

No! I cannot condemn this Man, for I find in Him no guilt. I cannot,
I dare not, condemn the innocent!

CROWD

Crucify him! Crucify him! Death to the false Messiah!

PILATE

Bring me water! You compel me by your violence. Take Him away and crucify Him! But know! I wash my hands of it. I am innocent of this blood.

Pilate washes his hands.

CROWD

We take it upon ourselves. His blood be upon us and our children!

PILATE

Therefore I, Pontius Pilate, pronounce this sentence of death on Jesus of Nazareth. But I have no share in this blood-guilt. It falls upon you, and your children. Now, take Him and crucify Him!

Enter the German Officer, dressed in uniform, along with Hitler.

GERMAN OFFICER

If you please, terminate the Passion temporarily in order to welcome our guest and honored friend.

Time stops.
A spotlight on Hitler.

HITLER

(To the audience, a private moment) Do you know who I am? You will think, perhaps, years later, that you know me from black and white colors. But black and white are not colors, although they are useful things. I have a strong desire to tell you about the colors—I was once a painter, you see—how one of my eyes has flecks of gold swimming in the brown . . . the people, they fell in love with my voice, but the women, they fell in love with my eyes—The dark protects us. Our eyes are the same color in the dark. Well.

I do so love public speaking.

Let me tell you about this village. The old man who played Christ was in his sickbed; a new Christ has stepped forward.

He looks at Eric, with approval.

The old must make way for the young, see. Plants and animals know this—people, stupid and crass—they cling to the vine.

I have come to a chorus of glad cheers. The people are always very glad to see me.

EVERYONE
(But for Violet and the Visiting Englishman, who abstain) Heil!

Hitler turns toward the crowd. They fall silent.
He works himself up into a public rage.
The following text is a quotation from Hitler's remarks.

HITLER
One of our most important tasks will be to save future generations and to remain forever watchful in the knowledge of the menace of the Jews. For this reason alone it is vital that the Passion Play be continued at Oberammergau; for never has the menace of the Jews been so convincingly portrayed as in this presentation of what happened in the times of the Romans. There one sees in Pontius Pilate a Roman racially and intellectually superior, there he stands out like a firm, clean rock in the middle of the whole muck and mire of the Jews.

Now, continue with your holy play. How I *love* the theater.

The Visiting Englishman snaps a picture. A bulb flashes.
On with the play.
Eric on the cross.
Heavenly choir music from Part One.
Eric looks up, sanctified. He has a glow upon his face.
Elsa and Mary 2 lament at the foot of the cross.
Hitler watches.
The sound of a train whistle and a train speeding across tracks.

Scene 16

Dearest Harriet,

I am writing to you by train. Forgive me if my penmanship suffers. The Passion was glorious. The young man who played the Christ glowed with some invisible spirit. I daresay it almost made me a convert. Don't worry, dearest, *almost* is the operative word. I am Anglican to my bones.

They had an odd little visitor to the play. Herr Hitler. Made me quite jumpy. Reminded me that I much prefer to stay out of politics and seek shelter in the sanctuary of art.

I long to see you, dear—you and the English countryside at the height of summer, when the light appears to last forever—and one can read out of doors until eleven o'clock! Why hunger for more than that?

SCENE 17

The Foot Soldier and Eric in the forest.

FOOT SOLDIER

I got my orders to leave.

ERIC

So soon?

The Foot Soldier nods.

Where are you going, exactly? Do they tell you?

FOOT SOLDIER

To Austria, to Poland, to Belgium, to France, to Russia. *(Pause)*

Good-bye, little Christ.

They kiss.

ERIC

And one for Belgium.

Eric kisses him on the neck.

And this one for Poland.

He kisses him on the ear.

This for Austria.

He kisses him on the hand.

And this for France.

He kisses him on the mouth once more.

FOOT SOLDIER

That was most definitely France.

ERIC

And for Russia.

He kisses him on the forehead.

Come back safely.

The sounds of war.

SCENE 18

Violet sits in the forest. She is older now. The sky is red. She holds her white ribbon.

VIOLET

My white ribbon looks red in the dark. I will scatter my bread crumbs and so find my way home.

A bird enters.
It is Carpenter 1, dressed in his angel wings from Part One.

Hello! Are you a talking bird or a silent bird?

The bird is silent.

Will you fly me out of the forest, bird?
Poor bird. Your body is too big to fly.

The bird blinks.

Maybe you're hungry. I have a few bread crumbs. Do you want them? You do. All right then. Peck the crumbs out of my hand. I'll remember my way home. I have to sleep now, bird. Will you watch over me while I sleep? Thank you.

She goes to sleep. The bird leaves.
Eric enters wearing a Nazi uniform. He sits beside her for a moment.
She wakes up.

Oh—you startled me. You've got a new costume.

ERIC

Yes.

VIOLET

It's ugly.

ERIC

I have to take you with me.

VIOLET

Where?

ERIC

I don't know.

VIOLET

Do you remember when you were in the play? How you let me out of a box?

ERIC

That was a long time ago.

VIOLET

Well, you're a man now. Why are they taking me away?

ERIC

You're not a native Oberammergauer.

VIOLET

I lived in the village my whole life.

ERIC

It's different.

VIOLET

Different how?

ERIC

You have different blood.

VIOLET

Jesus was a Jew.

ERIC

Kind of. But not really.

VIOLET

Do you remember your lines from the play? Many shall come in my name saying "I am Christ" and shall deceive the multitudes. For false Christs and false prophets shall rise. The sun shall be darkened, and the moon shall not give her light. Take heed. Watch and pray; lest coming suddenly He find you sleeping.

ERIC

You have a good memory.

VIOLET

Yes. I do.

ERIC

I'm sorry. We need to go.

VIOLET

Let's play a game. It's called would you rather. Would you rather kill a dog or kick a baby?

ERIC

How hard would I have to kick the baby?

ERIC

Kill a dog, I guess.

VIOLET

So hard that her head was dented.

VIOLET

Would you rather be deaf or poke someone in the eardrum with a needle so that they became deaf? It's a hard one, isn't it?

Eric nods.

ERIC

Poke someone in the eardrum, I suppose. It would be terrible to be deaf. I love music. Come on, now. We don't have time for games.

VIOLET

Please, before you take me, tell me just one story. Tell me the story of Little Red Riding Hood.

ERIC

Well, there was a little girl, wasn't there? She went to visit her grandmother, and her grandmother was a wolf. The wolf ate the little girl.

VIOLET

Yes—that's right. The Englishman didn't know the ending.

ERIC

Will you come with me now?

VIOLET

I always liked you. You don't have a jolly fat face like the other villagers—you always looked a little bit sad.

If the struggle against evil could be contained in one commonplace phrase, "thank you" is the only one allowed to Eric for the moment.

ERIC

Thank you.

A pause.
He extends his hand to take her away.

VIOLET

Wait. Right now—it's not like being in a play—no one's watching—you could do something different.

ERIC

They watch all the time.

VIOLET

Even so—even if they watch you every second of the day—even if they give you a costume and boots and a hat—even then you're not in a play! You're a man. And a man must decide for himself what he wants to do!

ERIC

Look—I can't talk to you. They're waiting. Let's go.
Now, take my hand.

VIOLET

No!

ERIC

I'll have to carry you then.

A physical struggle between them.
He picks her up.

VIOLET

Please don't.
I'd rather walk.

He puts her down.
They are still, facing out.

Epilogue

The rest of the cast enters the stage.
They look at Violet and Eric.
They look at the audience.
The sound of a train speeding across tracks.
Eric gives Violet a final push forward, into the light.
The lights change from red to grey.
A terrible silence.

Intermission.

PASSION PLAY

PART THREE

Spearfish, South Dakota, 1969–the present

◆

CHARACTERS

P	plays Pontius Pilate and Satan (was Pontius the Fish Gutter in Part One)
J	plays Jesus; P's brother (was John the Fisherman in Part One)
MARY 1	plays the Virgin Mary (was Mary 1 in Part One)
MARY 2	plays Mary Magdalen; Mary 1's sister (was Mary 2 in Part One)
VA PSYCHIATRIST	also plays ensemble roles (was Visiting Friar in Part One)
VIOLET	Mary 1's child, three years old when we first meet her (was Village Idiot in Part One)
CARPENTER 1	also plays ensemble roles (was Carpenter 1 in Part One)
CARPENTER 2	also plays ensemble roles (was Carpenter 2 in Part One)
DIRECTOR	(was Director in Parts One and Two)
YOUNG DIRECTOR	(was Machinist in Part One)
PRESIDENT REAGAN	also plays Queen Elizabeth and Hitler

There is some flexibility in terms of how to cast the ensemble roles; one of the Carpenters or the Visiting Englishman could play the Young Director, for example. The special effects guy could be played by the Machinist (which makes sense thematically); but if one of the Carpenters or the Visiting Englishman is more suited to the role, so be it. However, it seems important that the Visiting Friar become the VA Psychiatrist in terms of the transition toward secular confession in the modern world . . .

SET

Open space.
The suggestion of a tollbooth.
A horizon line.

1970: Spiritual need as there never was before. The turning away from God and modern man's flight before the world to come have in this world led to perplexity, helplessness, and resignation, to a fight of all against all . . . Man wanting to be like God and to redeem himself by his own strength has failed deplorably. Is this the reason why scores of people flock to Oberammergau?

—DR. KARL IPSER,
Das Passions Spiel Oberammergau,
official illustrated catalogue, 1970

Act One

◆

One: Prologue

ENSEMBLE

Spearfish, South Dakota, 1969!
Picture red earth
dead tribes
knickknacks, ghost towns—
big signs for miles
telling you, something's comin'—
the corn palace—
a real palace made entirely out of corn,
that's right, corn—
Ever been to the badlands?
You could go crazy
one stretch of rock looks
just like another stretch of rock.
In French the badlands means something like
this land is not so good for living in
but not many people speak French out here anymore.
Keep going, keep driving—
You'll pass the Battle of Wounded Knee
wasn't really a battle, more like a massacre—

it snowed a lot that day—the blood got covered up.
Drive past the Harley convention,
people riding with their beards
flapping in the wind.
Keep going, keep driving—
you're smack dab in the middle of this country—
the Black Hills all around—
then you'll hit exit twelve:
the Passion Play of South Dakota.

Two: 1969 — Backstage

Backstage at the Passion Play
after a performance.
J, who plays Jesus,
and P, who plays Pontius Pilate.
They're brothers.
They're taking off their costumes
and their makeup and drinking cold sodas.
It's hot out.

J

People were crying today, front row. I was glad, for your last one.

P

Till I come back.

J

That's what I meant.
Mom wants everyone up at the house tonight. Everyone's real proud.

P

Yeah. You'll look after Mary when I'm gone, won't you?

J

'Course I will.

P

I wanted to give you something before I left.

He gets out a reel to reel.

J

Music?

P

No, I recorded the wind. On top of the mountain.

J

You're always doing something funny.

P

I thought maybe you could use it, for concentration—help you study.

J

Uh—thanks.

P

So, what are they teaching you—up there at the university?

J

Philosophy.

P

Who you at now?

J

Saint Augustine.

P

Aw, Saint Augustine. Good stuff. Gotten to the part where he goes to the hooker?

J

I'm behind.

P

Well, he goes to a hooker.

J

But he's a saint.

P

I know. But he repents. That's the whole thing—he repents.

J

I bet they have hookers overseas.

P

I'll be thinking about Mary.

J

I know. Just kidding.
Look—thanks for the wind thing.
I mean it. I'll miss you.

P

Don't talk like that.

A crowd enters, all dressed in Biblical costume.

CROWD

Surprise!
For he's a jolly good fellow, for he's a jolly good fellow, for he's a jolly good fellow, which nobody can deny!

P

You didn't have to do this!

Mary 1 enters in her Virgin Mary costume.
She carries in a cake with candles.

MARY 1

Make a wish.

P

It's not my birthday.

MARY 1

But your birthday'll be over there. We're celebrating early.

P

Okay.

He blows the candles out.
P and Mary 1 kiss.

Wanna know what I wished for?

MARY 1

It's against the rules!

P

Okay, I won't tell you. I'll show you.

He gets down on his knees.

Will you?

MARY 1

Did you plan this?

P

Got the ring right here!

He takes the ring out of his Pontius uniform.
Queen Elizabeth enters, slow, silent.

Everyone suspends,
P kneeling before Mary 1.

THE QUEEN

My loving people.

I am resolved to live or die amongst you all, to lay down, for my
God, and for my kingdom, my honor and my blood. For I am married to England!

She takes P's ring for a moment.
She considers the ring. She puts it on her wedding finger.

We shall shortly have a famous victory over the enemies of my God!

Queen Elizabeth places her hand on P's head as he kneels.

Go forth into battle, my son, and go with God!

She places the ring on Mary 1's finger.
She moves to exit.
Mary 2 snaps a polaroid. A flash.
The scene continues as before.

P

(To Mary 1) Take that veil off!

She does.
He kisses her.
Everyone finishes singing:
"For he's a jolly good fellow, which nobody can deny!"

Queen Elizabeth slowly processes across the stage, waving to the crowd.
She exits.
No one notices.

THREE

A backstage tour, out of time.

MARY 2

(To the audience) That was the day everyone remembered. The day Pontius Pilate proposed to the Virgin Mary. Here's a polaroid I snapped—see, Pontius Pilate is kneeling down . . . proposing to my sister backstage.

I play Mary Magdalen. I'm not much of an actor. I do the play because I believe in the message. It's a message of love. Questions?

Questions from the backstage tour ensemble:

ENSEMBLE 1

Have you acted anywhere else?

MARY 2

Nah. I don't like the city. I like being in a place where you can see the horizon. I like to see what's coming at me. Even if it's bad.

ENSEMBLE 2

Who's that? *(Pointing at an imaginary photograph)*

MARY 2

That's a picture of my father. He started the Passion Play in America—
he didn't like how things were going over in Germany. He audi-
tioned over one hundred women for the part of Mary Magdalen. He
hired my mother. She was a vaudeville actress from Chicago. They
got married and my father—uh—upgraded her to the Virgin Mary.

ENSEMBLE 3

Did they play Christ and the Virgin Mary the whole time they were
married?

MARY 2

Sure did.

ENSEMBLE 3

Was that weird?

MARY 2

No, it wasn't weird. It was just how it was.

ENSEMBLE 4

Do you have a day job?

MARY 2

When I'm not in the play I work at the tollbooth out on highway
sixteen. The night shift. It's not the most glamorous job in the
world. But there's not a lot of jobs out here, not right now.

ENSEMBLE 4

Isn't that dangerous?

MARY 2

Oh, nah . . . I like to think of myself as a beacon of light on a dark
night. Funny, huh? Sometimes I press a quarter into a stranger's
hand in the middle of the night and think it's kind of like commu-
nion. Who knows if they get it. They just drive off, into the night.

Four

Mary 1 and P.
Mary 1 wears a bathrobe.
P is dressed in uniform.

P

When your alarm clock goes off in the morning, imagine it's me telling you I love you. Beep beep beep I love you.

MARY 1

Okay. I brought you this to keep in your pocket.

P

The Virgin Mary.

MARY 1

Yeah.

P

So I can keep you in my pocket.

MARY I

Yeah, me and her.

P

Bye.

He picks up an army bag.
He kisses her.

MARY I

Bye.

He leaves.
She waves.

FIVE

Mary 1 and Mary 2, in bathrobes,
helping each other put on makeup for the show.
Mary 1 is dressing as Eve.

MARY 2

Hold still. You got a smudge.

MARY 1

Thanks.

MARY 2

He's gonna be fine.

MARY 1

I know.

MARY 2

So buck up. You gotta put yourself in God's hands.

MARY 1

I hate to sleep alone. My feet get cold. I put socks on and then my
feet get hot so I take them off under the blankets but then my feet

get cold again in the night. It's unnatural, cold and unnatural, this solitary sleeping.

MARY 2

Maybe you should get a cat. When I'm cold I just put a cat on my feet.

MARY I

I'm allergic, remember?

MARY 2

Oh, yeah. I think allergies are so weird, don't you? Some people are allergic to their own skin. Why would God create allergies?

MARY I

Maybe God didn't create allergies. Maybe they just happened.

Mary 2 shrugs.
She makes a final touch to Mary 1's makeup.

MARY 2

God created everything. Even bad things. Right? You're ready to go on, babe.

Mary 1 walks onstage.
An ensemble member playing Satan, dangling an apple, approaches her.

ENSEMBLE

Eve. Eve.

MARY I

Who is there?

ENSEMBLE

I—a friend—and for thy good is the coming. Bite on boldly, be not abashed.

MARY I

I'm sorry—it's just. It's not the same as my husband does it.

Six

Mary 1 alone, in her bathrobe.
The sound of wind.
She is afraid.
J enters.
She jumps.

MARY 1

Thanks for coming. I got scared. The wind's so loud. Banging around—sounds like other things. I saw a snake today out back.

J

What kind?

MARY 1

I don't know.

J

Did it have a triangle head or a square head?

MARY 1

Didn't get that close to it.

J

I'm sure it was harmless.

MARY I

Didn't look harmless.

J

You want me to just sit here while you sleep?

MARY I

Okay. Only I can't sleep.
I made some hot chocolate. Want some?

J

Sure.

She goes to get it.

MARY I

(Shouting from off) How's school?

J

Pretty good.
I'm taking some acting classes, actually.

MARY I

(From off) They have acting classes? At the university?

J

Yeah.

MARY I

(From off) Why would you study acting out of books?

J

We get on our feet too. Today we imagined we were smelling lemons.
It was amazing.

Mary 1 enters with the hot chocolate.

I actually smelled a lemon and there was no lemon there to smell.

MARY I

Huh.
Well, I don't see why you'd study acting at a college.
You already know how to act.

J

Kind of. What we do is community theater, Mary. We all have other jobs.

MARY I

You want to have acting be your *job*?

J

Yeah.

MARY I

Where? New York?

J

Or Los Angeles.

MARY I

On television?

J

Sure. What?

MARY I

I just don't picture you on television. That's all.

J

Why not?

MARY I

Because I know you. You're not supposed to know people on television.

                                        J
Someone has to know them.

                                   MARY 1
I guess.

                                        J
You want some fancy cigarettes?
Might help you sleep better.

                                   MARY 1
I don't smoke that stuff.

                                        J
You mind if I have a little?

                                   MARY 1
No. You smoke that a lot?

                                        J
Not very often. Just in the afternoon, mostly.

                                   MARY 1
Hope you don't do it before the play.

                                        J
I think Jesus would appreciate really good marijuana.

                                   MARY 1
Oh, God.

                                        J
He was a peaceful man.

                                   MARY 1
Shut up.

He takes out a joint and begins smoking it.

J

Any letters?

MARY 1

Just got the first one.

J

What's he say?

MARY 1

Nothing about boot camp. Only those crazy made-up stories he likes to tell.

J

Read it.

MARY 1

I don't know if he'd want me to—

J

I'm his brother!

MARY 1

Well. Okay.

She takes out a letter from her bathrobe pocket.

Dear—Oh, I—I'll skip over that part.
Um—
Once upon a time there was an iron who fell in love with a wrinkle.
It was a tragedy. The end.
Once upon a time there was a lightbulb
who fell in love with the darkness.
It was a tragedy. The end.

J

He's crazy, my brother.

MARY I

Don't say that.

J

In a good way.

J exhales.

MARY I

Smells interesting.

J

Sure you don't want some? You're all wound-up. You'll be up all night.

MARY I

Maybe I'll try one little bit. Can't hurt.
Don't tell your brother.

J

I won't.

She takes a drag, smoking it like a cigarette.

Here—like this. That's how they do it in Woodstock.

He shows her how to smoke it like a joint.

MARY I

How would you know?

J

I've seen pictures.

MARY I

Oh.
So.

J
So.

MARY I
Today, after I did my snake scene, I saw a snake. In the backyard!
Isn't that weird?

J
Yeah, that's the reason I came over, remember?

MARY I
Oh, yeah. I forgot. *(She laughs)*

The weird thing is that while I was looking at it, it was pretty, not
scary at all. It was only *after* I saw it I was scared. What's scary
about a snake is not the Bible stuff—I think it's that a snake doesn't
have legs and arms and still it can kill you. I'm not afraid of bears
because you can *wrestle* with a bear, you understand how it thinks,
how it wants to hit you 'cause it's angry. But how can you understand something with no arms and no legs that wants to kill you—
no wrestling, no holding each other—just one bite and it's gone.
Your whole life.

J
You're stoned.

MARY I
No, I'm not.
Must be the hot chocolate.

J
Right. Don't you have that wind tape? Supposed to help you sleep?

MARY I
I don't like the wind. It makes me afraid.

J
What are you afraid of, d'you think?

MARY 1

The wind makes me feel lonely.

J

I think I'm stoned.

MARY 1

Oh.

J

You're stoned too.

MARY 1

I'm not stoned, I'm loney.

J

You're not loney, you're stoned.

MARY 1

I'm not loney, I'm stones.

J

That's right, you're stones, loney.

They kiss.

MARY 1

Wait. Who are you?

J

I'm just the guy who came over to stop the wind.

They kiss some more.
The sound of a gunshot.

SEVEN

P, in his uniform, drags a huge, bloody fish across the stage.
He holds a smoking gun.
A smear of blood across the stage. A red sky. Elizabethan fish puppet music.
A bright light—

P

My head!

P collapses.
Queen Elizabeth enters.

THE QUEEN

I cannot fathom why any subject would be willing to *die* for any
leader other than a *monarch*. What man would *die* for a leader who
was not *rushing* to the battlefield with him—their blood soaking into
the dust together. On the battlefield the monarch and the nation's
blood are one! *(She touches P)* Are you wounded, soldier?

P

I—I killed a fish.

174

THE QUEEN

May God keep you.
Carry him off the battlefield!
Now!

Big beautiful fish puppets enter.
The Carpenters, dressed as Elizabethan courtiers, carry P offstage on
an old-fashioned stretcher.
The Queen examines the smoking gun, curious.
She carries it offstage.

Eight

Mary 2 in her tollbooth, alone.
Night. Rain. Cars on the other side of the highway
pass by, their headlights across her face.
She sings a song to herself.
She sings to the tune of "Away in a Manger":

MARY 2

(Making it up as she goes along)
Away in a tollbooth
No room for his bed
No cars for an hour
To rest his sweet head—
I look for an angel—
I look for a—car
But no one comes by me
For hour upon hour.

Mary 2 looks out the window.
Mary 1 appears. Mary 2 is startled.

What are you doing here this time of night?

MARY 1

You busy?

MARY 2

Naw. No cars for an hour. You're soaking wet.

MARY 1

I had to talk to you.

MARY 2

Shoot.

MARY 1

If you thought you were——and you didn't want to be——what would you do? Would you get a—? What would you do?

MARY 2

But you're married. So it doesn't matter if you're—

MARY 1

I know, but just say I didn't want—

MARY 2

Mary, that's—

MARY 1

What?

MARY 2

A sin. Are you—?

MARY 1

I don't know.

MARY 2

Breasts? Vomit?

177

MARY 1

Yes.

MARY 2

Well, you're married. So—

MARY 1

I know.
But if I—would you forgive me—if I—?

Mary 2 nods.

MARY 2

You're my sister.

MARY 1

And you won't tell?

MARY 2

That I forgave you for something I don't know about?

MARY 1

Yeah.

MARY 2

No—I won't tell. But have you—already?

MARY 1

No. Thought maybe I'd get some kinda sign.

MARY 2

Mary.

The beams from a car approach.

MARY 1

(Thinking that it's a sign from the natural world) Oh my God—

MARY 2

Car coming. Duck down.

Mary 1 kneels down, making the tollbooth look almost like a confessional. A car approaches. We see neither the car nor the passenger, only light.

Here's your change, sir. Have a good night.

The car drives off.

I hate when they don't say good night.
No one's got any manners these days.

NINE

J and Mary 1 at rehearsal, the next day.
J on the cross.
Mary 1 kneeling down by it.

J
(As Jesus) Eloi, Eloi, lama sabachthani!

MARY 1
(As the Virgin Mary) Why, why is my son slain?

DIRECTOR
There needs to be more—um—anguish from both of you.

J
I just—I don't know if I can do this moment out of context.
Without the arc of the whole play, you know, to get me there.

DIRECTOR
The arc of the play.

J

Yeah. I'm serious. You have to go through the whole play to get there.

DIRECTOR

We can't run the whole show right now.

J

I know.

DIRECTOR

Then what are you suggesting?

J

It's just that—I've known these lines forever—and it feels stale—
and I'm sorry, but I don't feel like you're giving me any direction.

DIRECTOR

Is this what happens when you go to college? You turn into a prick.

J

I just want the play to be good.

DIRECTOR

Well. Me too.

J

So how do you want me to play this moment.

DIRECTOR

(Turning to Mary 1) Can you speak his language?

MARY I

(To J) You want it to feel real, right?

J

Yeah.

MARY I

Well, have you ever been betrayed?

J

No.

MARY I

That's too bad. Do you know anyone who's been betrayed?

J

Yes.

MARY I

Then why don't you use that.

DIRECTOR

Okay. That's fine. Use it. Let's go.

J

Eloi, Eloi, lama sabachthani!
No. It wasn't right. I wasn't feeling it.

DIRECTOR

It was better.

MARY I

No! It wasn't better! You're still *acting*! My father—he never acted—he just told the story. There was no—effort. There was no—acting.

DIRECTOR

It's not really appropriate for one actor to give another actor notes. If any direction needs to be given, I will give it. Now, let's try that again.

J

I don't want to rehearse this moment, okay? I'll get it right, in performance, when it happens.

DIRECTOR

Fine. Let's move on. Mary, let's have your line.

MARY I

(No emotion) Why? Why is my son slain?

DIRECTOR

Why don't you try rocking back and forth on that line. Hold your arms to your chest.

MARY I

(With no emotion, rocking back and forth) Why? Why is my son slain?

DIRECTOR

(To Mary 1) What's wrong with you?

MARY I

He's not even saying his lines!

DIRECTOR

If we can't get along in a *theater* when the world is falling apart then how can you expect anyone to get along in this world? There's a war on. Why don't you do it again. And think about *that*.

MARY I

I don't want to think about—

DIRECTOR

Now take a deep breath—

MARY I

But it's—

DIRECTOR

Then go.

J and Mary 1 take a breath.

J

Eloi, Eloi, lama sabachthani!

MARY 1

Why, why is my son slain?

DIRECTOR

Again.

J

Eloi, Eloi, lama sabachthani!

MARY 1

Why, why is my son slain?

Mary 1 weeps.

DIRECTOR

Again.

J

Eloi, Eloi, lama sabachthani!

MARY 1

Why, why is my son slain?

DIRECTOR

Okay.
*(To J) Y*ou can get down from the cross now.

J gets off the cross.

(To Mary 1) Can you repeat that in front of an audience?

J

Yeah.

Mary nods.

DIRECTOR

Good. It's going to be a long day. Take five minutes. I have to talk
to the lighting designer. We have to tech the ascension.

The Director exits.

J
Look, I'm sorry, okay. That never happened.

MARY 1
What never happened?

J
You know what.

MARY 1
Don't talk to me.

J
Mary, I've been in love with you since the seventh grade or longer and I'll never say another word about it.

MARY 1
What?

The Director and ensemble enter.

DIRECTOR
Lights up! Get on the platform!

J gets on the ascension platform.

Everyone in the tableau!

The ensemble makes the ascension tableau.

Can we hear the music?

Music swells. A reprise of the heavenly choir music from Part One.

Now, slowly move your arms up towards Jesus! In time to the music! *(To the crew)* More light! No we want it *back*-lit! On the scrim! More smoke! *(To J)* Are you rigged? Are you strapped in? Now lift him up.

J flies up.

Now the clouds part. The clouds part. Now look up at Him! Smile up at Jesus! That's right! Now everyone freeze! And—blackout.

Blackout.

ACT TWO

◆

ONE: PILATE COMES HOME

P hesitates outside a door.
Mary 1 enters.

MARY 1

You ready to come in?

P

Almost.
Can't believe it's you.
Let me just—

He traces her cheek.

Is it you?

MARY 1

It's me, honey.

She traces his cheek.
He winces.

P

Oh—

MARY 1

What did I—?

P

Don't touch me yet, okay.

MARY 1

Okay. Why don't you touch me?

He touches her hands.

P

(To the audience) She is a deer wrapped in brown velvet.
She is the air breathing inside the body of a violin.

MARY 1

What?

P

Nothing.
Sorry.
I'm not being myself, am I?
You know that funny phrase—what is it—remember me to your
mother. I need you to remember me—to myself. Can you—?

MARY 1

Think so.
Here we go—I'm remembering you to yourself.

She touches his forehead.
He winces.
Violet enters.

VIOLET

Daddy!

P

Violet!
The pictures of you were pretty.
But not half so pretty as you.

VIOLET

I drew you a picture of a bird.

She hands it to him.

P

Wow! How is it you can draw such a good bird, only three years old?

VIOLET

I'm good at drawing birds.

P

That's the best bird I ever saw. It's so good I bet it even flies.

He flies the bird picture around the room.
He picks up Violet and flies her around the room.

VIOLET

(Laughing) Put me down!

P flies crazier.

Put me down! I'm scared!

MARY I

You're scaring her, honey.

P puts her down.

P

I didn't scare you, honey, did I? We're just playing bird.

VIOLET

I know.

189

MARY 1

Why don't we all go to sleep. It's been a long day.

P

I'll sleep right here, just outside the door. You two call me if you need anything.

MARY 1

What? Why, honey?

P

So I can hear.

MARY 1

Hear what?

P

If anyone's coming.

MARY 1

No one's coming.

P

Not right now. But when we're *sleeping*. When you sleep outside you can hear the leaves if anyone's coming. I want to protect you. And Violet.

MARY 1

I know, honey. But it's safe here. It's South Dakota. Remember?

VIOLET

Why is Daddy sleeping outside?

P

To protect you from bad people.

VIOLET

Are there bad people tonight?

P

There are always bad people.

Mary 1 gives P a blanket.

Good night.
Sleep with the angels, Violet.

VIOLET

What's that mean?

P

Sweet dreams.

Mary 1 and Violet exit.

P curls up in his blanket.
He looks at the sky.
The sky is red.
He sits up.

(To himself)
Red sky at night, sailor's delight.
Red sky at morning, sailors take warning.

The chorus enters with wind machines
and Elizabethan boats.

They're coming through the fog to the shore, the tall ships, and I'm
making sure they get here safe . . . real safe . . . I feel a gale of wind coming from the north but I counter it with a gale from the south . . . I pour
wind into their sails, and it's important they get here by morning . . .

P steers the boats through the wind, conducting.
Violet enters.

You should be sleeping.

VIOLET

You should be sleeping.
Why are there boats in the sky?

P

You can see them?

VIOLET

Yes.

P

It's a secret, but your dad can control the wind.

VIOLET

Really?

P

Yep. See, when I was in the war I was the pilot of a ship.

VIOLET

And you blew the wind yourself?

P

That's right. So I could push my ship exactly where I needed to go.
That way, I never made a mistake.

VIOLET

When I was in the war, I was not a pilot.

The chorus exits.

P

What do you mean, honey? What war?

VIOLET

The war before.

P

Before what?

VIOLET

There is always a war before, and a war after.

P

Before this war you were safe, safe in your mother's stomach.

VIOLET

Nope. There was a war before. I died.

P

You shouldn't be thinking about wars. You're only a little girl. Get those wars out of your head.

VIOLET

You get the wars out of *your* head.

P

How?

She tries to pluck the wars out of his head with her fingers.
She puts the imaginary wars on the ground.

VIOLET

Now you.

He does the same for her.

P

There they are, two wars side by side.

They look at the wars.

Are they gone?

VIOLET

No.
Almost.
Jump on them.

They hold hands. They jump.

Two

J and P.
In the dressing room,
getting ready for rehearsal, putting on costumes.

J

You look good.

P

You look good too.
You need a haircut.

J

It's for the play.

P

Oh, yeah.
What ever happened to wigs?

J

I wanted it to look real.

P

Well, it looks like—real hair.
So.
I hear you been acting all over the place—summer stockyards?

J

Summer stock.

P

Good parts?

J

Pretty good. People think it's kind of funny, me playing Christ. They get a kick out of it, actually.

P

So it's—kind of like a gimmick?

J

I didn't say that.

P

Well what is it then?

J

It's just a—nothing. Look—there have been some changes in the play, since you've been gone. Mary write to you about it?

P

She wrote me about other things.

J

Well, there's a new director. A young guy. And it's more professional. There are more professional actors. And there's a real stage manager—not Hank from the garage. And there's a new sound system. It sounds pretty good, actually.

P

Actually. Since when do you say actually all the time—it makes it
sound like you think everyone else is a moron.
Sorry.

J

It's okay. Really, it's okay.

P

Wonder if I still know my lines.

J

My kingdom is not of this world.

P

Thou art a king then.

J

You still got it.

Three: A Rehearsal

P and J in costume.
Mary 1 and Mary 2 in costume.
Violet, dressed as a shepherdess.
The whole ensemble.
Including a brand-new director,
and a special effects expert.

YOUNG DIRECTOR
(To P) At this point, when you do the Satan bit, we're adding fire-crackers. So you sort of shoot firecrackers out of your arms, like this.

SPECIAL EFFECTS
They're regulation firecrackers. Completely safe. You just pull the cord, and whammo.

He shoots firecrackers out of his arms.
P winces at the firecrackers.

P
Sorry, I can't do firecrackers today.

YOUNG DIRECTOR

Okay, we'll work the firecrackers tomorrow. Let's move on to the second act. From: "I cannot condemn him."

P

(As Pontius) I cannot condemn him. What has this man done? Look at his face, so gentle in countenance.

ENSEMBLE

Crucify him! Crucify him!

P

I will do as you say. But look—I wash my hands!

P washes his hands. He sees blood everywhere.

Oh, there's so much blood . . .

YOUNG DIRECTOR

Hold on.
What's the matter?

P

Is this fake blood or real blood?

YOUNG DIRECTOR

It's water.

J

You okay?

P

It looks like blood.

YOUNG DIRECTOR

Maybe the water's rusty. Can we go on?

P

I, Pontius Pilate, at the desire of the whole Jewish people—condemn this man to death. Now, take him and crucify him.

Hitler appears.
P sees him.
No one else does.

HITLER

Do you know who I am?

P

(To Hitler) You'd better get out of here.

YOUNG DIRECTOR

Excuse me?

Hitler stands there, between P and the Young Director.

P

Sorry. What was I doing—washing the blood?

YOUNG DIRECTOR

That's right. Let's just take it from your line: I, Pontius Pilate—

P

I, Pontius Pilate, at the desire of the whole Jewish people, condemn—
Wait. The Jews are saying: kill Jesus! But they're religious men, right? And Pilate was a bad guy, a tyrant. How come they want to kill him and I'm being all heroic—like—no, no, I can't kill him?

YOUNG DIRECTOR

The Jews want to kill Jesus because He's too powerful.
That's how it's written in the Bible.
Isn't it?

MARY 2

Kind of.

MARY 1

We're just telling the story, honey, the story from the Bible.

P

Just telling the story, bullshit! Either the Jews killed Jesus or else they're innocent!

YOUNG DIRECTOR

Look, we've had the Anti-Defamation League here, haven't we?

CARPENTER 2

(To Young Director) Oh, yeah they came, about six years ago, and gave us some feed-back. Used to be we had horns on the costumes of the high priests but we took them off a long time ago—um—six years ago. So the Anti-Defamation League—now they really—um—like our play.

P

I don't care about a fucking league, I'm talking about a man, a real man.

YOUNG DIRECTOR

I think we need to get away from talking about the play as a real his-torical document and get back to the play as a *play*. It is our task as actors to—

MARY 2

It's not just a play! It's the word of God!

YOUNG DIRECTOR

Yes, of course. Can we move on now?

P

Move on, move on, who cares about anything as long as we move on . . .

YOUNG DIRECTOR
Look, I know you've had a
rough time of it,
but we only have one day
until dress rehearsal—

P
I don't want your pity,
I want to know what's going on
in this fucking scene!

(To Hitler) GO AWAY!

Hitler walks offstage.
The special effects guy assumes P was talking to him and backs away.

YOUNG DIRECTOR
Are you all right?

P
Yeah, yeah, I'm all right.

YOUNG DIRECTOR
Let's just take it from there—from: I, Pontius Pilate—

P
Okay. But I want to change it. I'm gonna say: I, Pontius Pilate, an agent of the State, condemn this man to death. Not the Jews, not history. *I* will take responsibility. Now take him and crucify him.

MARY 2
That's not what the Bible says.

P
The Bible says lots of things.

YOUNG DIRECTOR
Do you want to go outside?

P
I don't want to hit you.

YOUNG DIRECTOR

Then don't hit me.

A silent moment between P and the Young Director.

Let's take it from your line.

P

I, Pontius Pilate, an agent of the State, condemn this man to death. *I will take responsibility.* Now take him and crucify him.

ENSEMBLE

Oh, happy day for the people of Israel! Long live our Governor, Pontius Pilate!

YOUNG DIRECTOR

(To P) Thank you. Now exit stage left.

P looks left and right, forgetting what stage left means.

Double time, soldier.

P passes by the Young Director.
P clocks the Young Director.
A brief tableau.

FOUR

Mary 1 and the Young Director, who has an ice pack on his cheek.

YOUNG DIRECTOR
I'm going to have to fire your husband.

MARY 1
Look—give him another chance.
He just got home. He's not himself.

YOUNG DIRECTOR
I'm trying to put on a *professional* production—

MARY 1
—of the Gospel. You know how it'd look—in this town—if you
fired a soldier?

YOUNG DIRECTOR
How?

203

MARY I

Bad. 'Specially you just back from Canada.

YOUNG DIRECTOR

I'll give him one more chance. One.

MARY I

His understudy's out in Oklahoma anyway.

YOUNG DIRECTOR

He's not in Oklahoma, he's in "*Oklahoma!*"

MARY I

What?

YOUNG DIRECTOR

Forget it.

Five

The sky is red.
P, alone, on an abstraction of a roof, or a mountain,
assembling jars full of wind.
He stacks them.

P

Red sky, at night, sailor's delight.

He takes a jar, traps some air, screws the lid on.
Mary 1 appears.

MARY 1

What are you doing all the way up here?

P

I wanted some air.

He traps some more air in a jar.

MARY 1

You mean—as in—to breathe it?

P

Yeah. And to keep it. Here—
the night air. Perfect, like you.

MARY 1

Thanks, honey.

P

Look how red the sky is.

MARY 1

It's probably just the—nuclear reactor—next town over.

P

Maybe.
Or something bigger.

They look at the horizon, holding hands.

So, there was some stuff that wasn't in my letters.

MARY 1

You don't have to tell me.

P

I want to.
I was powering a ship that had a gunner on the back. And there were
lots of explosions—all the time—felt like they were right here.
(Pointing to his head) But one time, we heard this huge explosion, and
we heard people screaming, so we went ashore to help out. I was
holding a little girl—maybe Violet's age. Her head was in my
hands, and it was wet, and I realized her whole skull was—gone—
and her brains, in my hands—on my clothes—and for a long time
we thought the enemy shot into the camp, because we thought who
would kill women and children like that—but later I realized no—
we were shooting into the woodline. It was us.

MARY 1

It's not your fault.

206

P

There were no showers, you know—we were in country on February 28th—I didn't shower until May 10th. I washed my hands without water:

He rubs his hands together.

Pontius Pilate—with no water.

MARY I

Honey.

P

And I would think of old Pilate, lying there in the dark. How Pilate had good intentions—he *had* to kill someone innocent, it was all part of the big plan. He saved us all, didn't he, by being willing to be bad. But—a little girl's brains—there's no plan for that.

MARY I

You're a good man.

P

Yeah, right.
I don't want to be in the play anymore.

MARY I

What? Why not?

P

I don't believe in God anymore.

MARY I

It's okay—a lot of people don't believe in God these days—

P

No—it's not okay! In this town—people *should* believe in God—or else they're fucking hypocrites! You believe in God, don't you Mary—

MARY I

Yes, I believe in God—

P

Tell me you're the same, you're the same—

MARY I

I'm the same, honey, I'm the same—

He kisses her.

P

I still have the Virgin Mary in my pocket, see?

He shows her.

Six

A rehearsal.
The whole company.
Carpenters working on the cross.
Violet is dressed as a shepherdess.
The acting style is broad, gestural.

P

(As Pontius) Art thou the King of the Jews!

J

(As Jesus) Thou sayest so.

P

Hearest thou not how many accusations they hurl at thee? Why art
thou silent?

J

My kingdom is not—
Wait, can we stop?

YOUNG DIRECTOR

Okay.

J

I was thinking about this scene. And I thought it would be better if we toned it down. Just—real. Two men talking.

YOUNG DIRECTOR

In an amphitheater for six thousand people.

J

Could you mike us?

YOUNG DIRECTOR

We can hardly see your faces. Look—we need the physical *gesture*.

J

Well, I don't want to do it this way, this grand gesture stuff. It's fake. I want to do it for real.

P

For real.

J

Yeah, for real.

P

What do you mean real?
It's not real.

J

I want people to feel the *humanity* of it.

P

Are you saying how I'm acting isn't human enough?

J

I'm not saying anything about your acting.

P

Sure you are. You're saying I'm not real enough

J

I—

P

You don't need to pussyfoot around me, for fuck's sake, just say you
don't like the way I'm doing the scene.

A moment of danger.

J

Yeah, I don't like the way you're doing the scene. Actually.

P

What the fuck do you know about real? You want real?

J

Yeah.

P

You want real?

J

Yeah.

P finds a nail onstage, and a hammer, by the cross.

P

This nail is real.

J

Stop it.

P

This wood is real.

MARY 1

Calm down, honey.

P

And my hand is real.
You want to know about real sacrifice?
It's in the body.

P puts his left hand on the cross, palm up.
He holds a nail with his left fingers and points it toward his palm.
With his right hand,
he hammers the nail into the palm of his hand.
The world goes into slow motion.
The women scream.
Mary 1 turns Violet's head away.
P doesn't scream.
Blackout.

Seven: 1984

A clinical feeling. P and a VA psychiatrist at a VA hospital.
P's left hand is limp, crushed, at his side.

VA

What year is it?

P

October.

VA

What *year* is it?

P

Oh.

VA

It's 1984.
Who's President?

P

The actor.

VA

President Reagan, good, that's right.
I see in your records that you had a suicide attempt about ten years
ago, that you were hospitalized for a month in a South Dakota VA.

P

It wasn't a suicide attempt.

VA

No?

P

No. I crucified Pontius Pilate. I figured why not crucify the bad guy
for once, you know?

VA

You're the bad guy?

P

No, I played the *role* of a bad guy. It's a metaphor.

VA

It says in your records that you were given medicines for delusions.
Are you still on medication?

P

Ran out.

VA

I spoke to your wife on the phone today.

P

Ex.

VA

Okay. Ex. When's the last time you talked to your ex-wife?

P

Probably talked to her today. This morning.

VA

She said she hasn't talked to you in a year.

P

She doesn't talk to me but I talk to her.

VA

She mentioned that you think you can control the wind?

P

Did she?

VA

How do you know that you can control the wind?

P

The Lord told me so.

P smiles.

Just kidding.

VA

Do you think you can talk to God?

P

I talk to him but he doesn't talk to me.

VA

Well, that's a common enough problem.

P

I guess.

VA

Your wife also said you wanted to kill the President.

P

Nah. He's a good President. He gave me a raise. Three hundred dollars. Spent it on cigarettes.

VA

It says in your records that you've been in ten different cities at ten different VAs over the past ten years. You seem to travel a lot. Why'd you leave home?

P

I like to sleep outside. Look—I didn't come here to confess my sins to you. Unless you can absolve me of my sins, and I don't think you're qualified to do that, and I don't see any holy water in your office, just give me a pill, a pill for my troubles, a pill please. I have a really big king-sized headache. I thought about shooting myself to make my headache go away but I thought you might have like a really really big aspirin.

VA

I'll see what I can do.

He looks down at his chart.

P

Is this all we've got now? A bunch of white coats? No priests to say yes, son, your suffering meant something, no kings on the battlefield to say yes, soldier, your suffering meant something. Just give me a pill, a God-shaped pill, please.

The VA psychiatrist looks up from his chart.

VA

I'm trying to help you.

P

Yeah, thanks. Sorry. Look—I just want to get myself back to South
Dakota.

VA

And what'll you do when you get there?

P

I'll play Pontius Pilate the way he was meant to be played.

VA

And how's that?

P

Like a hung-over politician in a God-forsaken province who took
stupid orders on a really fucking bad day.

Eight

P pressed up against Mary 1, kissing her.

P
(Almost incomprehensible) Kiss me harder, into my heart . . .

He kisses her.

MARY 1
I'm your ex-wife, goddammit, wake up—

P
I just need somewhere to sleep,
honey.   MARY 1
                                     You've been drinking—

I just need a shower—

MARY 1
My God! You can't just *pop in* every couple of years and take a
shower here! How do you think that is for Violet? You could go to
the church—

P

I don't need a church. I need soap. And a razor.

MARY 1

What for?

P

Pontius Pilate didn't have a beard.
He was a Roman. He was clean-shaven.

MARY 1

There's no rehearsal honey—
there's no Pontius Pilate—
Someone else has it now!
A professional actor.
From Nebraska.

P

I'm going to talk to the director—
get my part back—

P

Oh, really a professional?

MARY 1

That's right.

P

From *Nebraska?*

MARY 1

He went to school—he's Equity—I don't know.

P

Is he better than me?

MARY 1

He's fine.
Yeah, he's good.

P

Really. Can he show what it's like to give orders to kill a man?
Unless he's been there and seen what it's like up close—

MARY 1
(Overlapping with his "up close")
Yeah, yeah, up close—
I've heard it before—
You can't stay here.   P
Where the hell have you been?   I killed people—for that
                                 man—and no one wants
                                 to give me a fucking bar of soap!

MARY 1

What man?

P

The President, who else.

MARY 1

There's another President in the White House now, honey.

P

Take your pick! A likeable man becomes a tyrant just like any other
man. In a democracy—likeability is tantamount to tyranny!

MARY 1

Tantamount?

P

Tantamount.

MARY 1

You're drunk.

P

No—I'm not drunk! In a democracy, it is a *likeeable* man who gets
elected. It is a *likeable* man who sends you to your death. What's the
difference.

MARY 1

There's a difference between a—a—likeable man and an evil man.

P

I can tell you, you don't *feel* the difference, when everyone gets zipped up in a body bag, and no one says anything about it, they just say "ZIP!" Because when there are guts—where skin should be—and skin, where guts should be—there's no difference between a nice guy and an evil guy who sent you out to kill. One of them is *photogenic*—the other one isn't—they both take you and they go ZIP.

MARY I

I'm sorry for the bad things that have happened to you.

P

I don't want your pity.

MARY I

Then what do you want?

P

A shower.

MARY I

One night.

P

I won't touch you, honey!

MARY I

(Leaving the room) Don't call me honey!

P

And could I please borrow a toothbrush?

She leaves the room.
She throws a pillow and blanket into the room.
She throws a toothbrush into the room.
She throws toothpaste into the room.

221

She shuts her door.
Violet enters.

Violet!

> VIOLET

I crawled out the back to see you.
Did you get my bird pictures in the mail?

> P

Yeah. You're getting real good with the bird pictures.

> VIOLET

I've been learning about the architecture of feathers. The way they're put together—layer upon layer. From the time of dinosaurs and angels. There is no homologue for feathers, that is to say there is no biological structure that resembles feathers. They came of themselves to the world because the birds needed them. But no one knows what came first, the bird, or the feather, or flight.

> P

What grade are you in now?

> VIOLET

Sixth.

> P

There must be a God.

> VIOLET

Why'd you come back?

> P

I want my part back.

> VIOLET

Someone else has it now.

P

I heard.

VIOLET

Then why'd you come back.

P

To see you.

VIOLET

Then why'd you leave?

P

I had to.

VIOLET

Oh.
Can I see your hand?

P gives her his hand.
She drops it up and down, limp.
She kisses his dead hand.

P

Thanks.

J enters.

What are you doing here?

J

What are you doing here?

P

I'm on a visit.

J

I'm on a visit too.

223

P

Kind of late in the evening for a visit.

J

Yeah, Violet, you should be in bed.

VIOLET

Don't tell me what to do.

P

Thought you were in New York, L.A., something like that.

J

I was.

P

So what are you doing here.

J

They wanted me back for a benefit performance of the play. The President's here, campaigning. He's going to watch it.

P

Really. You're doing the play for the President of the United States. Pretty fancy. It's my lucky day. I've been meaning to talk to the President.
Don't they put you up at a hotel?

J

Yeah. But I'm sick of hotels. Thought I'd see if the couch was available.

P

I reserved the couch.
Mary went to bed.
You want me to wake her up so you can say hello?

J

No.
I'm gonna head back to the hotel.

P

No. Stick around. Tell me about your life.
You married? Have kids?

J

No.

P

Why not? Famous actor, good-looking . . .

J

Look, where the hell have you been, you could have called, told
someone where the hell you landed.

P

No one wants to read letters from me.
I'm crazy, didn't they tell you?

J

I didn't need an expert to tell me that, actually.

P

Oh. By the way, I don't care that you've been fucking my wife, *actu-ally*. You should know that.

J

Violet, go inside.

VIOLET

No.

J

Don't talk like that in front of her.

P

Ignore the curse word, Violet.
I'm making a larger and more important point:

love's more important than fucking. That'll be important for your teenage years.

(To J) Do you agree that love is more important than fucking?

J

Yes, it is.

P

So you admit it then!

J

You want to talk about love? You selfish piece of shit. You want to talk about love? I've been supporting this family for the last ten years.

P moves toward J.

P

Yes, I want to talk about love. I'm dying to. Brotherly love. Christ's love for his disciples! Mary's love for her child! And the most glorious—the most profound love of all—the actor's great love of himself! You vain puffed-up little turd! Come here!

P grabs J. A scuffle.

(Over the scuffle) Am I my brother's keeper?
Am I my brother's keeper?

J

No, you're not!

VIOLET

Stop it! Stop it!

They suspend.

Did you know that orca whales are the only species who kill each other for fun, besides human beings? Did you know that Dad?

226

P
No.

J
No.

P

What?

MARY I

Who's out there?

P

It's only the wind.
(To J) Good night.

VIOLET

(To J) Good night.

J

(To both) Good night.

Nine: The Play

The tail end of "The Star Spangled Banner," sung by the ensemble.
Ronald Reagan with a hand over his heart, in a spotlight.
The song ends. Reagan waves his cowboy hat, and settles the crowd.
He gives a public speech:

REAGAN

Why, hello everyone. It's morning in America. Isn't it? I believe it
is. The dawning of a . . . new dawn. But, make no mistake, Armageddon is coming. With metal horses and tanks and a red sky.
I intend to stop it. God has a plan for me. I was once a lifeguard on
the Rock River you know. Saved seventy-seven lives. If the tide is
too much for you, I will save you.

I was at Mr. Gorbachev's over there in Moscow. His son's goldfish
died. I replaced it. You think history is made by great wheels set in
motion. Well it is. But it's also made by small acts of generosity.
I replaced a little boy's goldfish and a wall came crumbling down.
Mr. Gorbachev, tear down that wall!

Bob Hope once said what's it like being President and I said, it's like being an actor. Only you get to make up the lines yourself. Well, that's not really true. Mr. Gorbachev, tear down that wall! How's that sound?

My fellow Americans, we are a God-fearing nation. And God loves this country. Yes, He does. But we are in need of a great spiritual revival!

Cheering.
A light from the camera. A close-up shot.
A pivate speech.

I always liked the light from the camera. The light would go on and I would relax. All I saw was the light.

People say I wear a little rouge on my cheeks. It's not true. When I am laid to rest my cheeks will be rosy still. My campaign manager said what can we do to get those ratings up. Get shot again I said. It was a joke.

You know what my first job was? A radio announcer for baseball games in Chicago. And you know what? I never even saw the ball games. The games were in Chicago, I was in Davenport, Iowa! They would telegraph the plays to me, and I would make the folks feel like they were there, even though I was—elsewhere! That's what a great leader does. You don't even need to be at the game!

Cheering. A public speech.

Yes, this country is in need of a great spiritual revival. A brighter future for—everyone. Now people have said I'm not concerned about the poor, about the homeless. Not true. They're homeless, you might say, by choice.

He winks.

Now you're about to see a play about those values our country holds dear: family, God, and baseball. No, not baseball. God. And family. And intact families like Jesus, Mary and Joseph. And God, the Father. Two fathers, I know, but not really two fathers like that, not in that way, no, because those two fathers have the plague and will bring Armageddon down on the pure wheat fields of this land.

He smiles.

It's morning in America. We *are* that city shining on a hill. We are a people chosen by God to settle a promised land. You are that promise. We are that promise. And now, I give you, the greatest story ever told.

Reagan waves and takes his seat. The play begins.
It is now more of a musical. Very professional.
They sing a song.

ENSEMBLE

I will go
To the Father
And sit at His right side.
I will go
To the Father
The world to glorify.

MARY 1

My son! I must see you before you go away.

J

Mother, I am on my way to Jerusalem. The hour has come when I must offer myself.

MARY 1

Oh, my fears are terrible—

J

My hour has come.

MARY 1

I will go with you, even to death!

Mary 1 is acting better than she ever has in her life.

J

Be comforted. I will rise again.

MARY 1

Ah, God, give me strength that my heart does not break!

Reagan watches.
He wipes tears from his eyes.

Mary 1 and J embrace, full of love.
It is an odd extended moment.
They look into each other's eyes,
less like the Virgin Mary and Jesus and more like lovers.

P, from the audience:

P

Mary!

The scene suspends. Time stops.

(To the audience) Ever get the feeling
that you want to run onstage?
You want to move,
but you can't?
It's this horrible feeling,
as though you will run onstage
and speak lines all garbled—
lines you made up yourself?

REAGAN

(To the audience) I began to think of baseball.
Making it feel real for the crowds.

On the radio.
Bottom of the ninth.
The wind is *gusting* at Wrigley Field.
And now, the wind-up. And the
pitch—

P

This big stage
this stage of history,
this little block of wood
separates you from your most terrible fantasies—
it's important, this piece of wood, this stage, between you and it—

Reagan stands.

REAGAN

Batter swings—and it's a long fly ball to left field—and now my telegraph goes dead—it's dead—and I have to make it all up myself—it's a long fly ball, ladies and gentlemen, and it's going, and it's going—and it's gone!

The crowd goes wild.

P

Mary!
Stop the play!

Everyone onstage finally hears him. People are frozen.

Well, hello Mr. President.

Reagan salutes P.
P salutes Reagan.

REAGAN

I never did serve in the military, but I feel as though I did. I made training films for soldiers during the war. It was one of the happiest times of my life.

Reagan salutes P.
P salutes Reagan.

What's the matter, son? Dontcha have a part in the play?

P

No, Mr. President, I don't.
Mary, I love you.
I always did.

P pulls out a gun.
A secret service agent leaps for P.
P points the gun at himself.
Blackout.

Ten: Epilogue — The Present

Lights up on P,
whose left hand is limp at his side.

P

You might think, at the very end, that I'd kill my brother. Kill myself. Kill my ex-wife. Big love triangle, bang bang, an American Passion Play. But that's not how the story ends. I sat in my seat, and whispered: Mary, stop the play, and an old woman next to me said: shh.

I left the theater that day. Every month I take a bus to a different city. I sleep outside. That way I can hear the wind.

I send part of my disability check to Mary every month. She gives backstage tours at the theater. They replaced her with a professional actor. Sometimes I watch my brother on television. He's on a soap opera. I can read what happens to his character in line at the grocery store. They have these—little magazines.

I have a P.O. box. Violet sends me pictures of birds. Every year since she was a kid they looked more and more like real birds. Then she went to college, became a painter, and since then, every year, they started looking less and less like real birds. She looks like my brother but she's crazy like me, so who knows.

I started to believe in God again lately. Something about the light at night on a Greyhound bus going by a tollbooth. I think God is a tollbooth worker. Only he doesn't give exact change. You hand him a dollar, he gives you a fish. Go figure.

I don't know if this country needs more religion or less of it. Seems to me everyone needs a good night's sleep. That way we'd all wake up for real in the morning. It's good to be awake. When you're awake you can fight for what you believe in, no matter what costume you're wearing. Well. The more I talk the less you sleep.

I'll summon the wind for you, so you can sleep better.
(The good people at the VA hospital got rid of most of my delusions but I like to keep one or two around.)

Now: wind.
(He conducts the wind) From the south. To the west. There.
Good night. Sweet dreams.
Sleep with the angels, Violet.

The wind machines.
The boats. The courtiers.
Big, beautiful fish puppets.
The sky turns white.
P gets on an enormous boat.
He opens his left hand to the sky.
He sails off into the distance.

The end.

APPENDIX

◆

Some Notes on Set and Costumes

How to do essentially three different plays in one evening without losing one's mind and one's budget?

I think the designers need to think in terms of metaphor, transformation, and empty space. Rather than having eleven distinct costumes for all three acts, one might consider how an Elizabethan boot resembles a boot from 1969 and can be pulled through; or how a fish-gutting jacket in 1575 might resemble an army jacket in 1969, and how history bleeds through. The more successful productions were less interested in costumes looking historically accurate, and more interested in anachronism and simple homemade gestures.

In terms of the set using simple transformation to link the three worlds; at Arena Stage, Scott Bradley designed a succession of crosses in Part One that became telephone poles in an empty sky in Part Three. And when we did the play in Brooklyn at the Lafayette Avenue church, there was an open-handedness about the space and the set that seemed very right. Everything was in road boxes, and the road boxes became entrances and exits, wagons, things to climb on, prop closets, walls, etc. The props were designed with great care by Allen Moyer, but the church space was left raw, so that the scene where Mary 1 and Mary 2 are in the forest was played up against beatitudes which were gold-leafed on the wall of the church in the 1880s.

As for the boat that P gets on at the end of the play . . . at Arena Stage, P rigged himself into flying gear and ascended, with no boat. At the Goodman Theatre, where we had a fairly large budget, they constructed a massive boat that P got onto and sailed away. In Brooklyn, on our modest budget, we had a moving ladder (the large kind you hang lights with); and P climbed it, a sail was attached to it, and the chorus moved him offstage. I was very fond of the "poor theater" version in Brooklyn, as it allowed the audience to fill in the metaphor with their own imagination, and it used the simple tools of theater to create transformation: a little height, a little movement, a simple sail—and suddenly—an enormous boat.

To expand upon the lack of necessity for fancy scenery . . . On our first preview in the church in Brooklyn, a fire alarm went off. The audience was evacuated, as were all the actors, dressed in Biblical clothes on a windy night. After some milling around on the steps of the church, when it was clear we would all be outside for a while, the actors decided to go on with the play. First, Mary 2 sang a song about a tollbooth from the middle of Part Three, where we'd stopped. I thought perhaps we'd just have the song as an interlude; but slowly the audience quieted and gathered round, and somehow one after another, the actors came up and performed their scenes with no blocking, no props, no nothing, in silent agreement. A stage manager improvised a lighting cue with a flashlight, pretending to be a car; a cross was improvised with two actors hoisting up another actor, a sound cue was somehow found on a computer. I kept thinking one of the actors would stop, but in silent agreement, they simply kept doing the play. When boat puppets were called for, and a wind machine, the actors pretended to be boats, and made the sound of the wind. (I thought that once you got your Equity card, you refused on principle to ever make the sound of the wind again . . . but no, these actors made the sound of the wind). I was so moved that telling the story was more important to them than the fear of exposure. I suppose that's always the playwright's hope—that telling the story outweighs the very real fear of total public humiliation; but often there are things for actors to hide behind: costume changes, sound cues, beautifully painted drops, props, and the like. But on the steps of the Lafayette Avenue church, they had nothing but each other, the audience, and the story. And for half an hour, I was as transfixed as I've ever been, remembering that theater is, at its roots, some very brave people mutually consenting to a make-believe world, with nothing but language to rest on.

I tell that story only to give designers permission to do perhaps less than they would think they would need in order to create three epochs. I also tell the story to encourage smaller theaters with smaller budgets to do the play in burnt-out factories, or synagogues, or churches, or out of doors, and not to be intimidated by the stage direction: "He gets on an enormous boat and sails off into the distance."

Two Scenes That Used to Be in *Passion Play* and Are No Longer in It

❧

I included the Shepherd and Shepherdess as they used to be important characters in Part One and Part Two and I couldn't quite stand
them being relegated to the dustbin forever. So do with them what
you will. And I've included "Spring Song" because we rehearsed
that song for every production, and for every production ended up
cutting it. But it became a strange talisman of building ensemble for
the play. Feel free to do the same.

Scene 7: The First Day of Spring

Spring Song. Everyone in a circle, dancing around a maypole.

MARY I
Lucky the woman with a sea
In her shell, lucky the man to drink it.

CARPENTER I
Lu-lucky the man with well-hung fruit
Lucky the wo-woman to eat it.

242

PONTIUS

(Aside)
The prettiest walk is the walk towards death.
It is so slow and deliberate.

MARY 2

(Sings dismally)
Lucky the woman with a sea
In her shell, lucky the man to drink it.

CARPENTER 2

Lucky the man with well-hung fruit
Lucky the woman to eat it.

PONTIUS

(Sings dismally)
And happy the skin of a frog.

MARY 2

(Sings dismally)
Oh and happy the skin of a frog.

EVERYONE

(Happily)
Dong ding dong ding dong ding ding,
This morning is light,
This first morning of spring.

Scene 3: A Shepherd and Shepherdess on a Hillside

A game.

SHEPHERDESS

You know, you seem quite familiar to me.

SHEPHERD

Why, you seem familiar, too.

SHEPHERDESS

Do you know what my old job used to be?

SHEPHERD

No. You haven't been a shepherdess all your life?

SHEPHERDESS

I have not. In fact, I was a cloud fairy. I stitched together the clouds with milk that I carried 'round in a little pouch and turned to cloud thread.

SHEPHERD

How very strange! I thought you looked familiar. Oddly enough, I used to be a star thrower.

SHEPHERDESS

No! A star thrower!

SHEPHERD

Why, yes. We used to hurl the stars with all our might into the sky, and it was a dangerous job, you know, because the stars got all hot and sticky. The strangest part about it is that I was in love with a cloud fairy way back when I was a star thrower. I wonder if you might have known her—she was the most beautiful cloud fairy in all of the heavens.

SHEPHERDESS

Well, that's certainly strange. Because I was in love with a star thrower way back when I was a cloud fairy. And it was a forbidden, forbidden love—star throwers were not allowed to mingle with cloud fairies—for which I got banished to earth, where I sit now, alone and forlorn, bereft of my star thrower.

SHEPHERD

Oh, poor dear.

SHEPHERDESS

Yes. The ways of the earth seem strange to me and I do miss sleeping on the clouds.

SHEPHERD

That's indeed a strange coincidence. Because the cloud fairy who I adored above all other women was banished to earth, and I followed her there, by hurling a star with my whole body downwards, and keeping hold of it until I fell to the earth. See this mark? This is where the star burned my poor hand.

SHEPHERDESS

Shall I kiss it?

SHEPHERD

Oh, yes.

SHEPHERDESS

Your hand seems very familiar to me.

SHEPHERD

As does your kiss.

SHEPHERDESS

Could it be that . . .

SHEPHERD

Could it be?

SHEPHERDESS

No, it's not possible.

SHEPHERD

Is your cloud fairy name . . .

He whispers a secret name into her ear, kissing her ear all the while.

SHEPHERDESS

Yes, yes it is! And is your star thrower name . . .

She whispers a secret name into his ear, kissing his ear all the while.

They kiss.
The Sky Turns Red.
She pulls away, frightened.

Look, the sky! Again, the sky!

SHEPHERD
Don't worry, dearest, I'll protect you!

They jump to their feet.
She holds on to his finger, and they look at the sky.

SONGS

Spring Song

Sarah Ruhl

Trad arr. Wing-Davey

Heavenly Choir

G.P. da Palestrina (1525-1594)

ACKNOWLEDGMENTS

When you have been working on a play for the past fourteen years, as I have on *Passion Play*, there are many people to thank. But the biggest debt of thanks is due to Paula Vogel, who encouraged me to write my first full-length play, which became the first act of *Passion Play*. She and I would sit at a little café in Providence on Wickenden Street called Café Zog and she would buy me a cookie and read ten pages of *Passion Play*. Had Paula not said: "I think you should write that play," with the characteristic gleam in her eye, I would now be dissecting the imagery of wax in the Victorian novel. I would never have had the strange audacity to write the first sentence of a full-length play. At that time I wrote primarily poetry and fiction, and Paula snuck *Passion Play* into the New Plays festival at Trinity Repertory Company. Seeing that production, directed beautifully by Peter DuBois, was what made me decide to become a playwright. I arrived at the production after a car accident on Hope Street where I blacked out, woke up, showed up to Trinity Rep down the hill, saw *Passion Play*, and then the next fourteen years unfolded. Thank you, dear Paula.

Three children and seven plays later, I'm still tweaking *Passion Play* to get it ready for a production in Brooklyn at a beautiful old church, produced by Epic Theatre. Along the way, here are the people who helped to birth this play: Molly Smith, who beautifully directed the first incarnation of all three plays and commissioned the third act along with Wendy Goldberg who was then at Arena Stage; Mark Bly who served as dramaturg there; Rebecca Brown who did many readings of *Passion Play* in New York. And these wonderful actors who helped greatly with the process at Sundance, Arena Stage, Brown University and Lincoln Center Theater: Jefferson Mays, Felix Solis, Howard Overshown, Amelia Campbell, Annabel Capper, Michael Cerveris, Alan Cox, Carson Elrod, David Greenspan, Marin Ireland, Polly Noonan, Keith Reddin, Thomas Jay Ryan, Daniel Talbott, Joaquín Torres, Rebecca Melsky, and I know I am forgetting to write some of you down who have been in and out of this play over the last fourteen years, I am so sorry and thank you! Thanks to the directors Howard Shalwitz, Shira Piven, Chris Fields and Scott Illingworth. Thanks also to Tanya Palmer for her dramaturgy.

I am so grateful to the brilliant Mark Wing-Davey, who had the patience and enthusiasm to direct four very different productions, from a production in London that cost two hundred pounds, to one in Chicago that cost quite a bit more, to one at Yale where I think we finished the play, to the site-specific one we're working on now. Dear Mark, thank you, and some day we will take "Spring Song" on the road. To Oskar Eustis for being the first producer of *Passion Play* at Trinity Repertory Company and John Emigh for being the first to put on Acts One and Two together at Brown University's Leeds Theatre. To Kathy Sova for her very fine editing. To Bruce Ostler, as ever. To Bob Falls for having the courage to do a second production of a difficult and large play, and to James Bundy for understanding that sometimes playwrights need a third production to finish their rewrites. And thanks to Zak Berkman for having the vision and patience to put on *Passion Play* in an old church in Brooklyn.

Thank you to my parents who always entertained my metaphysical doubts even while they sent me to Catholic Sunday school. Thanks to my husband for helping me to keep the home fires burning while I have been at rehearsals. Finally, thanks to Professor David Hirsch at Brown University who taught Holocaust Literature, knew Melville inside and out, and who said to me once about a paper: "I am surprised. I would have thought you would have written something larger." Dear Professor Hirsch, I hope this is large enough (at any rate it is long enough), wherever you are now presiding, somewhere in the ether entreating people or shades to be ethical, to be literate, and to be large.

SARAH RUHL's plays include *In the Next Room or the vibrator play* (Glickman Prize, finalist for the 2010 Pulitzer Prize; nominee for the Tony Award for Best Play), *The Clean House* (The Susan Smith Blackburn Award, 2004; finalist for the Pulitzer Prize, 2005), *Dead Man's Cell Phone* (Helen Hayes Award for Best New Play), *Demeter in the City* (nominated for nine NAACP awards), *Eurydice, Melancholy Play, Orlando, Late: a cowboy song* and *Passion Play* (Kennedy Center's The Fourth Freedom Forum Playwriting Award). Her plays have premiered on Broadway at the Lyceum Theater (produced by Lincoln Center Theater); Off-Broadway at Lincoln Center Theater, Playwrights Horizons, Second Stage Theatre; and regionally at Berkeley Repertory Theatre, Yale Repertory Theatre, the Goodman Theatre, Cornerstone Theater Company, Arena Stage, Woolly Mammoth Theatre, the Piven Theatre; as well as being produced at many other theaters across the country. Her plays have also been performed in England, Poland, Germany, Israel, New Zealand and Australia, and have been translated into Spanish, Polish, Russian, Korean and Arabic. Sarah received her MFA from Brown University, where she studied with Paula Vogel, and is originally from Chicago. In 2003, she was the recipient of a Helen Merrill Emerging Playwrights Award, a Whiting Writers' Award, and a PEN/Laura Pels Award; in 2006 she was the recipient of a MacArthur Fellowship. Her work is published by TCG and Samuel French, and she is a member of New Dramatists and 13P. She lives in New York City with her family.